Tomorrow Will Be Better

D1566862

Tomorrow
Will Be
Better

SURVIVING NAZI GERMANY

Walter Meyer

With the Editorial Assistance of Matt Valentine

Library of Congress Cataloging-in-Publication Data

Meyer, Walter, 1926–

    Tomorrow will be better : surviving Nazi Germany / Walter Meyer :
with the editorial assistance of Matt Valentine.

     p.   cm.
   ISBN 0-8262-1217-4 (pbk. : alk. paper)

   1. Political prisoners—Germany—Biography. 2. Meyer, Walter,
1926–   . 3. Ravensbrueck (Concentration camp) 4. National
socialism—Moral and ethical aspects. I. Valentine, Matt.
II. Title.
D805.G3.M488   1999
940.53'17431572—dc21   98-50224
                                            CIP

Designer: Mindy Shouse
Typesetter: Crane Composition
Printer and binder: Thomson-Shore, Inc.
Typefaces: Gill Sans Light, Impact, Gill Sans Condensed

To my parents

Contents

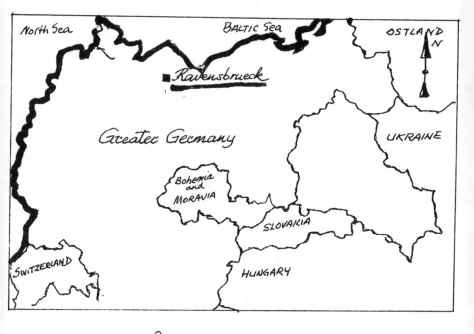

North Sea

BALTIC Sea

OSTLAND
N

■ *Ravensbrueck*

Greater Germany

UKRAINE

Bohemia
and
MORAVIA

SLOVAKIA

SWITZERLAND

HUNGARY

Ravensbrueck - 1945

0 ———— 150
MILES

(There were at least 35 *Subcamps*
administered by *Ravensbrueck*;
women's camps, men's camps,
mixed camps

Preface

"**Where are** you from?"

"When did you come to the U.S.?"

"What did you do during the war?"

These are questions I am asked frequently when people realize that I am not a native.

When I explain that I spent time in a German concentration camp during World War II, the question that follows is always the same: "Are you Jewish?" or, more positively, "Oh, so you must be Jewish!" Of course, my last name "Meyer," of Hebrew origin, could easily be Jewish. Many doubt me, simply because they are convinced that a non-Jew could not have been imprisoned in a Nazi concentration camp.

It's frustrating to me that the Holocaust has become an almost exclusively Jewish chapter in history. Few seem aware of the thousands of Germans, French, Russians, Poles, Italians, Belgians, Dutch, Czechs, the many Jehovah's Witnesses and the Gypsies, who were also prisoners.

The many books, movies, and monuments focusing on the

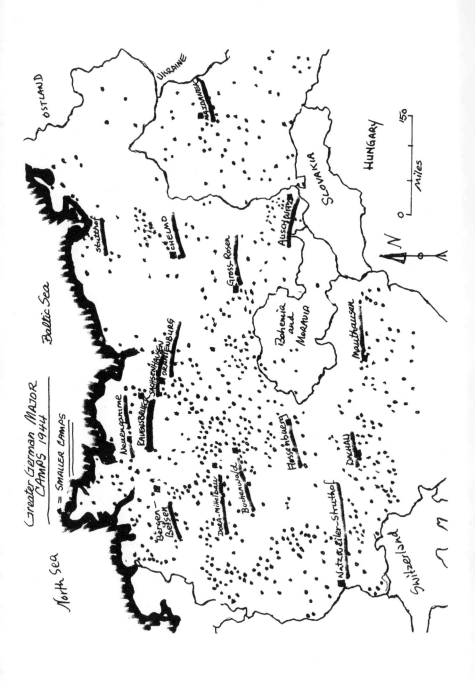

Greater German MAJOR
CAMPS 1944
■ = SMALLER CAMPS

North Sea

Baltic Sea

OSTLAND

UKRAINE

Stutthof

CHELMO

Gross-Rosen

Auschwitz

SLOVAKIA

HUNGARY

Neuengamme

Ravensbrück

Sachsenhausen
ORANIENBURG

Bergen-Belsen

Dora-Mittelbau

Buchenwald

Flossenburg

Bohemia
and
Moravia

Mauthausen

Dachau

Natzweiler-Struthof

Switzerland

N

0   150
└──┴──┘
Miles

Ravensbrueck Concentration Camp

1945 not to scale

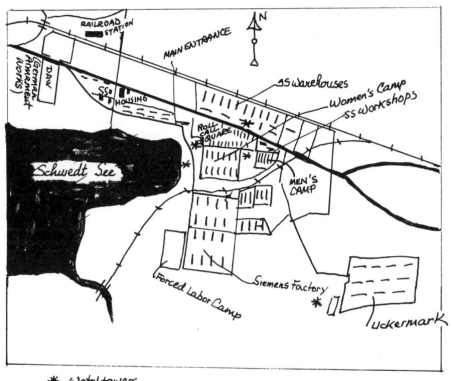

N

RAILROAD STATION

MAIN ENTRANCE

German Armament Works (DAW)

SS HOUSING

Schwedt See

SS warehouses

Women's Camp

SS Workshops

ROLL CALL SQUARE

MEN'S CAMP

Forced Labor Camp

Siemens Factory

Uckermark

* Watchtowers
+++ Railroads
— Barbed Wire
▬ Roads

Jewish Holocaust experience have helped to establish international awareness. For their part, Jewish survivors have been diligent and thorough in publicizing their ordeals and taking steps toward educating the world on this grim episode in human history.

The story, however, is as yet incomplete. When I tried to receive compensation from Germany for my imprisonment, I was told that I had missed the deadline. I explained that I had been in the Amazon jungle and did not know about any deadline. I even appealed my case to the German Bundestag. My case was denied. I can't help but wonder if things might have gone differently if I had been a Jew—if perhaps the seeming obscurity of cases like mine was somehow a license for this sort of mistreatment.

In my camp, Ravensbrueck Concentration Camp, 20 percent of all prisoners were Germans and Austrians (Austria had been annexed and its citizens were considered Germans), and 8 percent were Jews. Some of the camps had a majority of Jews, notably the infamous Auschwitz.

The Holocaust was the mostly successful elimination of Jews and any opponent to the Third Reich, regardless of race, religion, or nationality. There were hundreds of camps throughout Germany and the German-occupied lands. Only a few made the headlines. All were atrocious.

The men's camp of Ravensbrueck was headquarters for many small camps (Aussenlager) in northeast Germany. Thousands of prisoners worked in camps owned by large corporations such as Siemens and Heinkel, and never came to see the main camp. Camps Karlshagen I and II belonged to Ravensbrueck. They were located on the island of Usedom. More than two thousand prisoners worked there, assembling V-2 rockets.

Ravensbrueck was known as the Hetzlager—the rush

camp. Conditions were so horrible that prisoners who had come from Dachau Concentration Camp became homesick. Some prisoners worked on estates of high-ranking SS officers. Rutabaga soup became the staple food.

All of this information is available in library books, but the scholarly texts don't seem to satisfy the same persistent questions. So I go on answering them. I am frequently asked what my thoughts are with regard to the Holocaust and the killing of millions of Jews. I try to correct the inquirer and change the question to "millions of humans." There cannot be a justification for the planned liquidation and annihilation of religious groups and opponents to Hitler. However, I feel that it is more important to ask and to find an answer to *"why?"*

I have spent years trying to understand, and I have read many books. I have looked at the whole world rather than at Germany alone, and I find that most nations were pro-Hitler and anti-Semitic. The so-called civilized nations of the West stood by and watched in silence, often contributing directly or indirectly to the mass slaughter. Without the negligence and disregard of the Allied powers, especially the United Kingdom and the U.S.A., Hitler could not have succeeded with his "Final Solution." I accuse the world, and I can hardly cope with man's inhumanity to man. For further reading on the subject, I strongly recommend the book *The Holocaust Conspiracy: An International Policy of Genocide,* by William R. Perl (Shapolski Publishers, New York, 1989.)

Upon the question of whether I think that there could be another Holocaust, I have to say, "YES." If I look only at the evening news, I have no other choice. However, I am an optimist, and I recognize that it does not *have* to happen. Somehow, I hope that the intelligentsia will prevail and that we will seek the moral responsibility of the intellect to provide the leadership necessary for a free society.

And when I am asked what could be done to prevent a repetition of the Holocaust, I reply: "Education, not *quantity* but *quality* of education." Unfortunately, too many rulers are afraid of a literate society because literate people ask too many questions. One cannot, however, be free and ignorant at the same time.

The great Thomas Jefferson had enlightened ideas and ideals that many intelligent men have tried to implement. The late Professor William E. Drake, my graduate supervisor at the University of Texas, dedicated several of his books to me. I am certain that he would not mind that I copy the Addenda of his 1983 book, *Betrayal on Mount Parnassus* (Philosophical Library, 200 West 57th St., New York, N.Y., 10019):

> If Thomas Jefferson were alive today, he would be saying to us:
> 1. You have substituted an Aristocracy of Wealth for an Aristocracy of Intellect and Talent.
> 2. You are using your High Schools and Universities as mere training grounds for Professional Athletes.
> 3. You have so tied your ETHICS to Church Dogmas that you are incapable of Making Independent Moral Judgments.
> 4. You have become so Anti-Intellectual in your non-thinking that you are rapidly becoming Anti-scientific in policy decisions affecting the General Welfare.
> 5. You are so addicted to the Role of Power and Mechanization in your everyday life that you no longer sympathize with the Poor and Down Trodden.
> 6. Your Concept of Freedom as License has destroyed its significance as a Creative Force in Human Progress.
> 7. You have reduced the Free-Enterprise System to nothing more than a means of gaining Wealth at the Expense of Your Fellow Man.

8. You have so warped and distorted your Heritage of Freedom that it has become a Whipping Boy for Vested Interests.

9. You are so much a victim of Commercialized Ath letics that you no longer have any respect for Cre ative Labor.

10. Your ignorance of your Historical Culture has left you adrift in a Sea of Cultural Chaos.

11. Your Narcissistic Individualism has deprived you of the significance of the Social Self.

Acknowledgments

This book was started many times, and numerous written pages ended in the wastebasket.

Without the encouragement and assistance of many friends it would have been very difficult to complete the manuscript.

There is Walter Richter, always willing to listen and help. There are Lee and Kathryn, John and Lisa, Jim and Sally, Don and Maggie, William and Kay, Alex and Becky, David and Carilu, Matt and Teresa, Bill and Ann, Ola and Anne-May, and many more. Jos Baker in South Africa took time to offer editorial suggestions. Friend and survivor Dr. Bill Samelson edited the entire manuscript and gave valuable advice. Thanks also to Michael Gelb at the United States Memorial Holocaust Museum for his input. Matt Valentine, a most talented young writer at the University of Texas, spent many hours with me and is responsible for shaping the final edition.

My gratitude to Beverly Jarrett, Director and Editor-in-Chief of the University of Missouri Press. She lent me her ear and made publication of the book possible.

My wife offered me love, patience, and hope. Without her God knows where I would be and what I would do.

To all of the above many thanks.

Finally, thanks to all of those who, throughout my life, gave me a little warmth, some understanding, consideration, assistance, food, and a place to rest.

With so much help and encouragement I am ready for the next challenge.

Tomorrow Will Be Better

Prologue

I could feel the ground moving beneath my feet.

"Please," I said, leaning on the shoulder of a man next to me, "I need to sit down. I'm going to faint."

"That's a hell of a thing to do," said another passenger on the train, "pretend like you're going to faint so you can get a man's seat."

"This man really looks sick," another said. "Why don't you let him sit down? He's obviously been through a lot for all of us," he added, gesturing toward the *Wehrmacht* uniform that hung limply from my body.

One of the passengers stood up and offered me his seat.

It was February of 1945. I weighed about eighty pounds. People noticed my emaciated body; they stared at me on the streets and whispered among themselves as I passed them, but nobody thought my condition so extraordinary as to warrant an exclamation or an effort to help me. Apparently, they were used to seeing eighty-pound soldiers returning from the eastern front. German forces there had been cut off from their supply lines and had nearly starved to death before they were allowed to retreat.

No one suspected.

Looking at the people around me, I noticed an unnatural absence. There were children with mothers, children with grandparents, women alone, men alone—but not a single complete family.

There was a mystery behind every partial family. I looked at a little girl sitting near me who seemed to be by herself. I wondered where she was going and where she'd been. She looked at me, turning around suddenly and staring right at me, expectantly, a spark of hope in her eyes. I decided not to ask.

There was a mother three rows up from me. She was sitting in an aisle seat, and she'd caught hold of her son by the arm as he ran past.

"Sit still!" she said. "Why can't you stay put?"

The boy was an attractive child, probably about ten or twelve years old. He reminded me of myself at that age— athletic, an extrovert who only managed to keep himself out of serious trouble because people saw him as "cute" and couldn't hold a grudge against him for long. Just like me, he presented the unique dilemma to parents of being both irresistibly adorable and stubbornly bratty.

A haziness seemed to creep up on me periodically, blurring my vision into muted darkness and quieting the train sounds to an unintelligible droning in the background. I felt cold. In the darkest moments I'd think of my mother and of my home in Duesseldorf; then I'd remember where I was going, and my athlete's instinct would find again the pocket of inexhaustible stamina that kept me going.

Several times in the course of the previous two years I would have welcomed death. I sat up in the narrow train seat and looked at my wrists. The scars that ran across them had healed now, leaving thick, smooth, white lines as testaments to desperation.

It was worse in prison than in camp. By the time I reached the camp I was numb; nothing could affect me enough to produce more than a vague, delayed reaction. In prison, however, I was full of spark and drive. Beatings and isolation still bothered me, and bad food wasn't yet appreciated as a great alternative to no food. In the camps I had needed out, but in prison I had really wanted out, which made me dangerous.

I coughed into my hand. Coughing was terrible for me not only because of the burning in my lungs and throat but also because a violent cough could shake my whole body, making my joints feel as if they were coming unhinged. This cough had produced a lot of blood; I put a cupped hand discreetly into my lap.

I had tuberculosis and was expected to die.

I had been diagnosed in camp.

The other prisoners had cautioned me against going to see the camp doctor: an unhealthy diagnosis was likely to prove more fatal than the disease itself.

"What good is a sick prisoner who can't work?" they asked. "Why would they keep feeding you if you were too sick to meet your *pensum?*"

I wiped away the phlegm and blood on my pant leg and looked at my hands. My fingers seemed so much longer. Even here the flesh had deteriorated, making the long bones underneath more pronounced. I fell asleep staring at my fingers folding in upon each other, sliding away from me in the monotony of train sounds, gears turning wheels over miles of track, extending behind me, to Ravensbrueck.

The Old Country

She was a frail woman, nearly seventy, and it was with great effort that she raised the ax. She held the chicken in her left hand, pinning its wings to its sides. If the bird had any worries, it wasn't showing them—it sat quiescently on the block, its only motion the constant fitfulness of its head, darting here and there curiously.

Grandaunt had asked the men in the family to kill the bird, but no one was up to it—chickens were rare and valuable status symbols in the village, and this one, old as it was, remained an object of reverence among the members of the household.

And so it was my great aunt who had gone to the coop that morning. And it was Grandaunt, thin arms quivering, who brought the ax down on the bobbing head of the aged foul.

Who wouldn't die.

The weak stroke had broken some bones in the neck, but the bird was still alive and whole, and riotously alarmed. The two old girls fought it out for a moment, Grandaunt landing the occasional glancing blow with the blunt end of her weapon, and the chicken making a good show of it with a flourish of flying feathers and a few strong scratches from its scaly talons.

In the end, the bird got the better of the woman and wiggled free. Its neck had been bludgeoned so severely that the head flopped down at its side and, as it sprinted across the yard, it must have seen the world upside down.

Grandaunt chased it around the yard, giving up once she had exhausted herself.

The bird died a few minutes later, and we all ate chicken soup that evening without mention of the incident.

This was Hollerath, part of the old Old Germany.

It's been a long time now. I'm back in Hollerath on vacation, visiting family. Today my wife, Yim Ping, had her first sled ride.

It's still beautiful here. The winter air is still brisk and cold and fresh. Something is different, though. Everything changed so quickly. As a child I had the briefest glimpse of what things must have been like before industrialization and the wars reshaped the country—an echo of my father's childhood.

Born of peasant stock in 1890, he was a child of the country and later a man of the city. He grew up in Hollerath, a tiny village on the Belgian border where a man's wealth was gauged by the size of his manure pile and an inflated pig bladder in the window was an invitation to come in for some blood soup.

In childhood visits to my granduncle's house, I caught glimpses of the lifestyle my father must have had. I can remember meals eaten around a giant table, everyone circumventing the need for plates by gathering around a single immense frying pan and choosing a portion of its space from

which to eat. Family members would select a section carefully, mindful to include at least a sample of everything available, which usually included ham and bacon, eggs, potatoes,
some vegetables, and sometimes sauerkraut. Someone
would start a prayer, methodical and rich with the very
Catholic tedium of the era, and everyone would join in, picking up the lines like a choir singing a familiar tune. One of the
men who had been working hard all day might start to nod
off, but a quick shout from the matriarch would wake him up,
reminding him of his Christian duties.

Religion was important. No one was very concerned with
the ideology behind their beliefs, but everyone harbored a
sober fear of the final hour that kept them politely attentive
during religious activities. Leaders of the church were highly
respected, especially the local priest, who together with the
forest ranger and the chief of police formed a triumvirate of
village power that superseded anything else. (A political rep-
resentative was added in 1939, expanding the hierarchy with
a fourth leg.)

The deference allotted the priest reached far beyond
simple respect, elevating him to the position of someone
slightly more than human. My father recounted a childhood
memory to me once, in which he'd been walking with a
friend along a cow path and had seen the priest in the distance, urinating against a tree. The two boys were shocked,
since they were both under the impression that priests simply
didn't have to urinate. Eventually they admitted to each other
that what they were seeing was real, but agreed not to mention it to anyone else for fear of losing credibility.

My father had already had a rough time gaining acceptance
from the villagers. Before he was born, my grandmother had
been sent away to a village in the valley to work and look for
a husband, and had returned pregnant and unmarried. The

locals were so shamed and enraged by her sin that they formed a mob, ran her down, and threw stones at her until the local priest convinced them to stop, quoting John 8:7: "He that is without sin among you, let him first cast a stone."

Though she survived the mob, she had to give birth to my father in a hayloft.

Grandmother eventually married the man who had impregnated her, but life was only marginally better following the match. They were as poor, if not poorer, than everyone else in the village. Money was a rarity, so most villagers got what they needed through bartering or by making things themselves, continuing to do so until well into the war.

My boyhood visits were enhanced by the privations. Granduncle had two mules, named Fritz and Ella, that he had purchased from the army. I enjoyed being with the animals, and I felt important when put in charge of them, taking the mules to the water trough and keeping the cows from wandering into unfenced potato and oat fields.

There was a huge respect for farm animals—a lot depended on them. Most of the necessities came from cattle, which provided milk and cheese and fertilizer, pulled the plows, and dropped a calf once a year before finally giving up their hide and being turned into sausage for the dinner table. Everything bigger than a dog was shod and used as a draft animal.

The houses were low structures, kept small to conserve heat. Granduncle's house had a kitchen and dining area, two bedrooms in the attic, with the stable attached. Water came from a well shared by several households.

"Where is the water closet?" I had asked on my first visit. Everyone laughed at the question.

"Walter, we have no water closet."

"The outhouse then."

"There is no outhouse, either," Granduncle explained. "Use the stable."

Life was simple. No one cared whether I brushed my teeth, and the food was unequaled by city standards.

I can remember Grandaunt, with her wrinkled, strong hands, holding a loaf of freshly baked bread to her large bosom and marking the cross onto it with a knife, then cutting slices for all of us. It was delicious bread, very coarse and thick.

When my father was still a boy, my grandfather got a job in the Mannesmann steel plant in the valley. Since it was so hard to make a living as a farmer, many men sought work cutting logs or producing charcoal, and quite a few ended up at the plant—dozens of men could be seen riding their bicycles down the valley to work every morning, then pushing them back up in the evening. My grandfather was an ambitious and outgoing man, and it wasn't long before he was offered a promotion. The company wanted him to work at their headquarters in Duesseldorf, acting as "wagon master" transporting seamless pipes from the factory to the railroad station.

At twelve years old, my father had never been outside the village, and was reluctant to leave behind the animals and the rolling countryside in exchange for automobiles and smokestacks. Everything was foreign in the city—even the sky lost its brilliance and paled to gray.

Once he got into school, my father was immediately relegated to the back of the classroom, the traditional seat of dishonor. On a visit to the classroom, the school principal asked why the new student had been moved there.

"He's from the Eifel mountains," the teacher explained, "he's a little retarded."

Indeed, the boy could hardly speak a word of *Hochdeutsch,* proper German. Though it wasn't his fault—they spoke their own dialect in Hollerath, and no one had ever told him that people spoke differently elsewhere.

However, Paul Meyer, Jr., was just as ambitious as his father, and he was not about to back down from a challenge. Rather than developing his social skills like the other students at parties or in dancing lessons, my father spent his every free moment in the library. In a matter of months he had mastered German. That done, he went on to conquer French, English, Italian, Spanish, and Russian.

Meanwhile, the elder Paul Meyer was busy with pursuits of his own. Having come to a dead end in his career with Mannesmann, he changed directions and joined the police force. Though not quite so elite as their counterparts in the villages, Duesseldorf's police officers commanded the respect of the public, and none more so than my grandfather. He walked with conviction, bolt upright, his rather prominent belly decorated with a gold chain and watch, and sent the children scattering in fear as he approached. Toys were dropped as little boys and girls shouted out their warning, "Polizei Meyer is coming!"

In a local competition men pulled other men on roller skates to prove their strength, and my grandfather, boasting an impressive eighteen passengers, won the title "Duesseldorf's strongest man." Not long after, he captured the notorious "terror of Duesseldorf," a serial killer who had murdered several children. To increase his income, he volunteered for special guard duty on prison transports, a position no one else seemed to want. Almost daily, his reputation grew.

Everyone in the community respected the Meyers, and when my father joined the military and applied for a garrison in Metz (where he planned to practice his French), everyone wished him well, imagining that he would soon be commanding the German army. Indeed, father had ambitions of his own not far removed from those of his admirers back home. He was, however, inclined to delay his plans for a while in light of some newer developments.

Henriette Paula Sommerhauser, the extraordinary woman who was to become my mother, encountered Private Paul Meyer for the first time one afternoon as she was walking her dachshund.

My mother was beautiful and intelligent and kind. She looked at the world around her with constant wonder, appreciating everything. At the dinner table one evening she held up a chicken leg and remarked, "Look! See how similar it is to a human's leg?" Flowers and bright colors delighted her. In her mind, everything was beautiful.

The great tragedy of those childhood years was the death of my brother, Paul. At the age of sixteen, he ventured into the mountains to find some rare flowers for our mother. He slipped, and his body was discovered with a flower clutched loosely in one hand.

Despite their sadness, my parents were in love in those days before the war. The future looked bright for them. They could not have known what would become of their world, their country, or their surviving son.

From Altar Boy to Inmate

I was in the main police headquarters.

Having just received about a half-dozen lashes from a bamboo switch, my rear end was more than a little tender. I half-stood over the little wooden stool in the room, listening to the noises outside, wondering when my parents would show up to haul me home for another beating.

The banging from the hall was becoming louder. An SS officer was coming to fetch me, and the sound of his boots was ricocheting down the corridor and into the little room where I was waiting.

It was an impressive sound. In parades the SS would march down the street, dozens of them clicking their metal-studded heels against the ground and singing. They loved to sing. My childhood memories of the glory of Duesseldorf are marked with the thunderous rhythm of a hundred boot heels and loud, boisterous singing from the Nazi soldiers.

In solo the boots of the SS elicit quite a different connotation.

"Why did you take the shoes?"
"I don't know."

"Do you realize that the penalty for looting is death?"

I had been walking home after an air raid, and had helped myself to some shoes that I had found scattered across the street, leather shrapnel from a recently bombed shoe store.

Another officer came into the interrogation room and whispered in my interviewer's ear. They both left momentarily.

When they returned, they seemed much more upset with me. The first man sat in front of me and stared coldly into my eyes, while the second paced relentlessly back and forth across the back of the room.

"And were you with anyone before the air raid?" he asked, the tone in his voice suggesting that he already had an answer.

"Some friends. We were socializing."

"Liar!" he shouted. "You were with a group of boys planning subversive activities against the Hitler Youth! We know about your involvement with the *Edelweisspiraten,* and we know you sympathize with the French!"

I wanted to argue, to tell the officer that he had no right to accuse me of such things. Unfortunately, everything he'd said was true.

In 1940, at the age of fourteen, I had been required to join the Hitler Youth *(Hitler Jugend,* HJ), just like every other healthy German boy of the right ethnic background. There were several advantages to being a member of the HJ. The organization ran all of the recreational and social programs; if you wanted to play sports or go to a party, HJ was involved at some level. And being a member got us out of church, as well, since meetings frequently took place on Sunday mornings.

The Hitler Youth had evolved from the Boy Scouts, incorporating the discipline, camaraderie, and patriotism of the earlier program and adding elements of indoctrination and training that had practical military applications. *Jungvolk* (Young People), a preliminary program for ten- to fourteen-year-olds, served as a feeder to the HJ, but was focused more on recreation than premilitary training. I'd had a good experience in *Jungvolk*—I had made a few friends and learned how to play the drum for the little marching band. We were cute kids in uniform—everyone loved us.

The Hitler Youth was a different experience for me. It was regimented and organized—everyone had an assigned niche and was expected to fill it nicely. It was divided into five branches, each corresponding to a respective branch of the military. I was a strong swimmer, and so became a member of the navy branch.

A few years earlier, swimming competitions had been organized between various clubs. Now, everything was regulated by the HJ. So HJ Dusseldorf, section 6, would compete against HJ Cologne, section 7 and identical units in other cities. It was a giant playoff that ended with the *Reichsjugendmeisterschaft* (national youth championship), which had an indoor competition in Stuttgart and an outdoor meet in Breslau. Eventually, the scope of the contest grew to encompass the rest of the newly seized German territory and became known as the European Youth Swimming and Diving Championship. I attended two of those, one in Milan and one in Vienna. I was popular and successful, but I was miserable.

Perhaps there were a few insightful Germans who refused to participate in the Hitler Youth. I was not such a hero. I rebelled against authority, but I was motivated by a need for personal freedom rather than ethics. My father, on the other hand, disliked Hitlerism. I think the ridicule he received as a farm boy attending a big preparatory school taught him to dislike the type of exploitation that was allowing the Nazis to be as powerful as they were. Also, having been in every major battle of World War I, he knew that the Nazis wouldn't have much of a chance fighting against the Soviets, which seemed inevitable despite the promises of the Non-Aggression Pact. He was a moralist and a pragmatist. I was a pragmatist.

Still, there were some aspects of the program that seemed to me to be simply *wrong*. The Hitler Youth changed people's personalities. I was used to being a leader among the kids in my community—my peers respected me for my individuality and daring behavior. But as they became officers in the HJ, my old friends became obsessed with the artifice and the prestige of authority. The swastikas on their arm bands and the "Blood and Honor" slogan inscribed on their belt buckles seemed to lend them a new sense of arrogant bravado, making them tough and proud when in groups, but still just cowards on a one-to-one level. It was disappointing, really, because I had tried to instill in them a sense of adventure and of self-reliance, but they'd opted for symbols and catchy phrases rather than the real thing.

I disrespected them and showed it openly. When they addressed me with the "Heil Hitler!" salute, I didn't respond—a sign of disrespect of the gravest nature. I encountered a few like-minded boys, and we formed a little fraternity. We'd heard about a group in Berlin called the *Edelweisspiraten*— Edelweiss pirates, who were organizing against the HJ. We decided to start a Duesseldorf chapter, and went to work ruining or hiding HJ officers' bicycles, dirtying their uniforms, and doing whatever we could to foul up the typical order of things. (A favorite of mine was leaving condoms on the rear reflectors of their bicycles.) We were never political, as good-intentioned people would later claim; we just enjoyed throwing a wrench into the works to see what would happen, trying to get back at the corporal who'd made one of us do too many push-ups one afternoon. We managed to get away with it nicely for a while, just adding a little more chaos to an already chaotic setting.

By 1943 Duesseldorf was being bombed steadily. We were an industrial city, and therefore a primary target of the Allies. Food was becoming scarce.

The city did what it could to protect its factories. French prisoners of war were kept in the basement of a factory near my house to deter the bombers from hitting it. I was intrigued by these men, alone in the home of their enemy, facing attack from their own allies. I would sometimes sneak away at night and try to talk to them through the barred basement windows. I could hardly see them in the darkness, but I could imagine what they looked like—haggard and tired, frightened but brave. I was a source of some food and information about the war, and the questions they asked were always the same: Had America entered the war? Would they be released soon? What was happening in France?

I had already had some French in school, and I had enjoyed it. Taking advantage of the opportunity to practice the language, I talked with the prisoners for as long as caution warranted, developing a fluency that would prove invaluable after the war. The language practice was in and of itself enough to keep me going back every night, but the real reward was the drama of it. In a way I was like a spy.

One night, after I had brought the French men some bread and talked with them for a while, I went to a café downtown to meet with my buddies from the *Edelweisspiraten*. We were playing billiards and talking, and were just racking up the balls for another game when the sudden wail of an undulating siren cut off our conversation.

"Air raid," someone said.

A few moments later, the planes came through, blasting buildings and scattering debris on the streets. We could hear the huge engines of the bombers, accompanied by sharp explosions and lower rumbles as structures slowly toppled after being disheveled by indirect blasts.

After about an hour, it stopped. We stood in silence for a moment, waiting for a second wave. When another siren sounded, steady and unbroken, we knew that the bombing was over for the time being. We went out to have a look around.

It's fascinating to wander a newly bombed city; it always looks like a completely different planet. Nothing is as you remember it, almost as if the bombs had created a new city on the ashes of the old one.

On King's Avenue near the café we walked through a small field of broken glass that had once been the facade of a rather large shoe store. One of my friends and I quickly snatched up as many shoes as we could carry. I stuffed the shoes in my coat and the two of us went down the street to Adolf Hitler Square to examine our prizes under a streetlight. People were filing out of a nearby bomb shelter and wandering past us.

I unbuttoned my coat and let the shoes fall into my hands.

"They're all lefts," my friend said.

An elderly lady who had come out of the bomb shelter walked by and I tried to give her the shoes, but she was already a little confused and badly shaken. I pressed them toward her, but she wouldn't take hold of them. She kept shaking her head at me and pushing away.

"Take them," I urged. "They're good shoes."

"Leave me alone!"

"You! What do you have there?"

We'd attracted a police officer. I started running.

The officer shouted for help, and I found myself confronted by a human barricade of civilians trying to lend a hand. I tried to dodge them, weaving my way between the outstretched arms of well-intentioned civilians, only stopping when I found myself caught in the crushing grip of a hairy brute about twice my size who beamed with pride as he handed me over to the officials.

One period of my life had met its conclusion, and another, darker period was about to commence, beginning in the Duesseldorf police station and continuing unchecked through confinement, disease, and ultimately the Holocaust.

My arrest was only one of the many times I embarrassed and disappointed my parents. They didn't know what to do—they became stricter and stricter with no effect. I was told on many occasions that I was beyond hope, a "bad" child. I failed everywhere, at home, at school, even in church.

It wasn't that I didn't try. There was nothing more pleasing to me than the rare bit of praise I received for doing something right. Somehow, though, I could never stay out of trouble for long; I'd always botch things.

For example, I served as an altar boy when I was eleven, and my curiosity led me to interrogate the local priest about a variety of subjects.

"But why does everyone hate the Jews so much? Jesus was a Jew, that's what the inscription means: INRI, Jesus of Nazareth, King of the Jews."

"You must learn to accept Jesus as Jesus, my son," he said. My muscles stiffened when he called me "son." It seemed unnatural to be called "son" by this man. I didn't like him, and he didn't even know me. He had no children, yet he called everyone son.

I overturned the sacramental water that day on the

rectory steps. There was an audible "ooooo" from the audience as the holy water spilled over the church floor in a widening puddle of the Holy Spirit.

My misbehavior in school was even worse, though. It enraged my parents to hear that their son was one of the brighter students at school, but constantly started fights and ignored assignments. In light of my scholastic blunders and rambunctious behavior, my parents decided to send me to a boarding school in Mannheim. They thought that it would be better for me.

The school itself was at one end of the city, whereas the boardinghouse where we students lived was at the other. The house was a four-story dormitory: students on the first three floors, and the director and his family on the fourth. My roommate came from a wealthy family and always had money, which made him a good friend to have. The two of us got along fairly well, though my tenacity more than once got him into trouble.

Life at the boarding school seemed too restrictive to me. I was always looking for ways to make things more exciting. This ambition was to lead me in and out of tight spots for the duration of the war, but during those early days at the school in Mannheim, I was a physically mature boy striving to break free of the confines of tedious academia, and my mischief was more laughable than dangerous. I looked for opportunities constantly, and what I found, I took.

One day on my way to school I passed an attractive young lady. For an instant our eyes met, and we both realized that we were staring at each other. Her name was Elfriede, and she became my first girlfriend.

We weren't able to talk much, but we communicated by passing notes when we got the chance.

She was sixteen.

She asked me once in a letter how old I was.

"Seventeen," I lied.

She came and watched me occasionally during my physical education class. I was conscious of her once while I played *Schlagball* (hitball, a kind of baseball) with my friends. I would hit the ball, watch it bounce and roll away, then run. I could feel the weight of her infatuation as she watched me.

After the game, she gave me her address. After that, our meetings were more frequent.

My time with Elfriede seemed a stark contrast to the daily routine at the boarding school—being with her made me even more conscious of my surroundings. I can remember slumping onto a wooden bench and eating tasteless food while aromatic whiffs of the director's meal drifted down from upstairs, slowly permeating the building. While my classmates and I would sit, hunched over a bowl of something lukewarm and gray, the smell would float past us. We'd stop for a second, deciphering the aroma, detecting hints of delicious meats or warm pastries. After a seemingly endless frozen moment, someone would return to his food, and the lot of us would snap out of it and resume eating, angrily.

I was fairly sure that I'd be expelled from the school before too long. My roommate was in the same boat by association, but he lacked my vision for going out in style. Still, I was able to get him to help me execute a plan that would put us both in a lot of danger.

It was near some holiday, and the director's family went into a baking frenzy. Cookies came out of the ovens by the hundreds, though I knew from experience that none of them were intended for the students. The director and his family were going to be out for a while attending a theater function. I had about two hours.

I broke into the director's apartment.

It didn't take long for me to dump the cookies into a pillow case, and the subsequent rampage through the building was like a combination of Christmas and a good game of *Schlagball*—my excitement in distributing the cookies throughout the dorm was only exceeded by the adrenaline rush I got from all the running.

Everyone called me a hero, but I didn't get a chance to celebrate for very long before I had to make my escape; once the director got back someone was bound to tell him who'd done it. My accomplice and I had to make our exit through a third-story window, since the lower windows wouldn't open and the doors were locked from the outside. We climbed down via a rope we'd made from bedsheets, which we then buried in a garbage can in the alley near the dorm. We were ready to take off.

"I'm going to see Elfriede," I said. "Can you give me some money?"

He handed me a reasonable sum and then stood there, looking bewildered.

"We'd better get out of here," I said. "Where are you going to hide?"

He stared apologetically at the ground.

"I'm staying here," he said.

"You can't. They'll know that you had something to do with the cookies—and you've already escaped!"

"I'm staying. My father would be furious."

With that, he retired to the front entrance to wait for the director to return.

"Tell them I made you do it!" I yelled after him, but I doubted that he would.

I found my way to Elfriede's house and stalked quietly through the garden until I was close enough to hit her window with a well-aimed pebble. My second throw woke her up. She opened the window and stared out.

"Come on, let's go," I urged her.

She disappeared momentarily and then reemerged at the front door.

"Quiet," she said, holding a finger over her mouth.

She had left a note for her parents telling them that she would be back later.

It was after midnight when we found a small hotel. We took two rooms.

Social control had always been very effective in Germany. The police checked guest lists daily and examined them for anything suspicious.

At dawn, a plain-clothes policeman in his early fifties knocked on my door. I'd been up and waiting for him for half an hour.

"I'm trying to get some rest, officer," I explained. "My cousin and I were out at a party most of the night. The poor girl is pretty tired—I'd appreciate it if you could let her sleep."

I had prepared her for the police visit, coaching her in what to say and how to act, but the officer was satisfied with my story and left her alone. After he left, we spent the remainder of the early morning together.

Neither Friedchen (a pet name) nor I had had any experience in love-making. We trusted each other, however, and did our best to make each other feel good. I was a bit embarrassed when I had a premature ejaculation, but Friedchen didn't seem bothered by it. We kissed and held each other until we fell asleep.

I had enough money left over from what my roommate had given me to buy a modest breakfast for the two of us, and I promised to help her get out of any trouble that she might be in with her parents. I walked home with her, and we explained together to her mother and father that we had been out late at a party with friends from the swimming club, and had been scared to walk home so late.

"We spent the night with my friends," Elfriede said.

"We would have called," I added, "but there was no phone."

Her parents weren't upset—their daughter was a responsible young lady.

"I love you," I told her as I prepared to head for home in Duesseldorf. "I'll be back soon."

By that time, I'd spent most of the money I'd been given, so I couldn't afford a train home. I thought about hitchhiking, but I doubted that I could make very good time, and finding truck drivers headed in my direction might prove a little difficult. Thinking about hitching gave me another idea, however, which seemed to have better prospects. The Rhine was almost a straight shot from Mannheim to Duesseldorf, and the river traffic was fairly heavy at that time of year.

I went to the docks and made a few enquiries, and though most of the boatmen there had never really thought of taking on passengers before, most seemed willing to entertain the idea. The barge I arranged to travel with was to stop in Duesseldorf to pick up steel, then moving on to Duisburg, a common routine. I promised to be good and stay out of everyone's way, and the captain agreed to let me come along.

There's something unique about being on a barge. Many of the captains own their own ships, and live aboard and raise their children there, sometimes from birth. There was no work for me to do, aside from helping the captain's wife hang the laundry out to dry. The clothesline stretched from one end of the living quarters to the other, transversing a space that caught the wind brilliantly in a flash of bright banners of shirts and pants and pennant underwear. The captain's wife and I would follow the line, standing between the clapping thunder of a pair of trousers fighting a gust or a sputtering bra in a steady breeze, collecting all of it and placing it in a basket. We glided smoothly down the Rhine, letting the strong currents carry us toward Duesseldorf.

I often swam in that river as a child. In Duesseldorf, I would swim against the current, fighting it with my entire body, legs kicking with great thrusts of energy, arms clawing for purchase, lungs burning as they took in huge gulps of air. Finally I would reach a loaded barge, climb aboard, ride a mile or more, then jump off, letting the river carry me back downstream. I knew that it was dangerous: I once had to pay a visit to a woman in my neighborhood with the news that her son had drowned in the Rhine.

This time, I stayed on board and let the barge carry me all the way to Duesseldorf. When I got there, I searched out my friends.

"And you really stole the cookies?" one of them asked me after I had recounted my adventures.

"Mmm. Yes. And they were good."

It felt good to be with my buddies again. They respected me, and this latest episode had really gotten their attention. After a while, though, I got up the nerve to go home and face the consequences of my escape.

"Why are you like that?" my mother asked. "Why do you give your parents nothing but sorrow?"

She had already received notice of my escape via a very nasty letter from the director. My father was still stationed in France—he hadn't heard about the incident.

"You don't understand, Jettchen," I explained. "The director was no good. He was cruel; he feasted constantly while what we ate was terrible."

"Your father will be very angry," she warned.

"You don't have to tell him. Just tell him that I couldn't stand it any more and that I came home. You don't have to tell him about the director's letter."

And so it was that my father didn't discover my deviance in Mannheim for quite a while. He was, however, disappointed that I had dropped out of yet another school. The atmosphere was as usual unfriendly, so I tried to stay away as much as possible, only coming home to sleep, eat, and collect my mail.

Mostly to collect my mail.

At that time, the mailmen were all involved with the war, so we had women delivering the mail. Adele was more than your typical letter carrier. She was the kind of woman who got to know everyone around her (in my case more than others). A well-timed "hello" and a constantly pleasant demeanor kept her in favor with everyone on her route—she was easy to talk to and pleasant to listen to.

Being an adolescent male, and having wetted my sexual appetite, I pursued her, and was met with success. She was older and had had more experience, so my encounters with her were almost tutorial—at last a discipline in which I was willing to be educated!

My letters were delivered to me directly, instead of being put in the letter box, and I noticed that Adele was more than a little suspicious when she brought me a letter from Elfriede.

"Who is this girl who is writing you letters?" she asked.

"A cousin in Mannheim," I said, snatching the letter away from her.

When I was alone later I opened it, hoping to hear some

words of adoration from my Friedchen—she was thinking of me, she missed me—something like that.

Instead, I read her words with trepidation. "I am pregnant . . ." She was not one to delay the inevitable: ". . . and we need to talk." I did not continue, but instead put the letter in my pocket.

I was asleep when Mother collected the laundry, and of course she discovered the letter and presented it to my father, who happened to be in town at the time.

"Get up."

I pulled myself from sleep to face my father. It took my brain a few seconds to register what was happening.

My mother was hysterical. My father was stoically angry.

"Did you sleep with this girl? Did you have sex with her?"

I nodded.

There was considerable argument after that. My father was of the attitude that I should face the consequences for my actions alone, since I had gotten myself into the situation that way. My mother objected, pointing out that I was still just a boy, but in the end my father's outrage prevailed, and I was left alone to contemplate my future.

I spent the next few days trying to raise money to help Friedchen. She had decided to have an abortion, but still needed my support financially and emotionally. I gave her what I could.

The next news I received was from a hospital. Friedchen had gone to a back-alley doctor who had been recommended by a friend. The procedure had not gone well for her.

Under the circumstances, my father decided to intervene. He helped get Elfriede into a nicer clinic, where she eventually recovered from the injuries and trauma of her experience.

I think of her often, and of the child we could have had. I never saw her again.

The situation that I was in with Elfriede didn't do much to strengthen my relationship with my father. His philosophy that anything disagreeable in a child's behavior could quickly be remedied with violence was shared by thousands of fathers throughout Germany. It was, after all, just part of the pecking order. The church sanctioned the idea, as it had for centuries, referring to Old Testament passages in which the devil was "beaten out" of those who had gotten weak and ventured "away from the path," which could just as easily mean a boy who had ventured away from the path of cleaning his room as it could anything else.

And so it was that Hitler's offer came as an irresistible opportunity to Germany's youth. Here was the chance to escape the confines of traditional acquiescence—to wear a uniform and be in charge of something instead of always being told what to do and getting the hell kicked out of us every time we got out of line. Here was an opportunity to fight back, to do the beating instead of being beaten.

I was ecstatic, then, when I received an official-looking letter from the *Reichsjugendfuehrer* (National Youth Leader) inviting me to apply to the prestigious Adolf Hitler School. Acceptance was based on an individual's physical and mental achievements, and I was honored to have been noticed, though a little bewildered. I was ordered to report to Moenchengladbach, a city about twenty miles north of home, for screening. I doubted that my father would approve of it, but he was out of town, so I went.

I took a train with the other Rhineland candidates, and we spent a weekend at the *Jugendherberge,* a youth hostel. There were classes, questionnaires, films (Nazis loved films), physical examinations, and athletic events—my forte.

I was picked to compete in a boxing match, a sport with which I wasn't familiar, against an opponent who was at least two years older. Everyone formed a circle around us as we fought, mostly shouting encouragement to the big fellow who was using me as a punching bag.

"Kill him, Hans!" someone shouted, "knock his teeth out!"

He hit hard, but I was used to being smacked around, so I stayed put and endured it, landing a punch of my own when I could. After five rounds I was still on my feet, and the match was called a tie.

I had proved myself, and I was accepted. I'd earned the right to join the Adolf Hitler School.

My father wouldn't let me go. I hated him for it.

My father's implicit dislike of the Nazi regime was becoming a little precarious. He listened to the now-banned BBC and read foreign newspapers. He would talk among friends—in private, of course—about his quarrels with the hierarchy of the Reich.

"You shouldn't talk like that," friends would tell him. "You're liable to get yourself into a lot of trouble."

People were becoming as wary of what they believed as they were of what they said.

During the interrogation that followed my arrest for looting, my life was saved in part by the reputation of my grandfather, with whom the local police were familiar, and my father, who had won an Iron Cross in World War I. Also, some of the officers had heard of my accomplishments as an athlete, so my captors came to the conclusion that my situation warranted a little lenience, and they softened their attitude toward me.

Unfortunately, another problem surfaced after my transfer to Gestapo headquarters. There seemed to be some confusion about my penis. I'd had a lot of pain as a youngster since I'd had a deformity of the foreskin that wouldn't let the skin stretch out correctly when I got an erection. My first attempts at masturbation had left me wincing. The problem was solved by a partial circumcision.

I'd undressed for a strip search, and one of the Gestapo officers became a little suspicious. He waved at one of his colleagues.

"Come here, look at that," he said.

The two of them huddled around me, inspecting first my facial features and then my genitalia.

"Das ist ein Jude," one said.

They were unable to decide anything with certainty, however, so they called in a *Rassenspezialist.* The race expert listened to the reports of the other two officers, then started his own examination.

He was perplexed.

My partial circumcision was beginning to give me some trouble to compensate for the pleasure it had allowed me in the past. It seemed to me that they almost hoped that I was a Jew, preferring that scenario to the possibility that a troublemaker like me was a "real" German.

Eventually, however, my penis and I passed inspection.

The question of racial superiority seemed obvious enough to me—Germans were the master race, and Jews were the bane of the world. Certainly, there were confusing factors such as Jesus' Jewish origins, but these seemed somewhat trivial compared to the expansive evidence we were supplied with that showed us how the Jews had cheated and deceived their way into economic power. The Jews, we were told, were responsible for communism, poverty, and the Black Plague. My biology textbook in school outlined the traits of the Jew, using examples such as Marx and Trotsky as "typical Jews."

My own experience with Jews up to that point seemed to contradict the anti-Semitic rhetoric I learned in school; I had had Jewish friends as a child and was unable to recall any particular deviance on their part. There were the Froehlichs, Wallachs, Freundlich and Schwarz children, all of whom I had grown up with and played with as a child. Their parents always offered me cookies and other goodies. It was confusing for me when they all started wearing yellow stars sewn into their clothing. I felt somewhat alienated at the time since I was the only one among them who didn't have one.

They started disappearing not long after that.

It was getting scary. I didn't have any particular love for Jews, and I could recite from memory a hundred or more atrocities that had been attributed to them, but these kids were my *friends,* and that was different. Out of a sense of fairness, I decided to hide one of them in my basement for a while, a boy named Hans-Dieter Brandenburger. I didn't know him intimately, but we'd played together and he seemed like a nice person.

My basement sanctuary became unavailable when I was arrested for taking the shoes. Fortunately, a friend of mine took over for me and managed to hide Hans-Dieter for the duration of the Third Reich.

Hans-Dieter and several others that I had met were great kids, and we all knew it. Still, the children of Germany believed what they were told about the Jews. It really wasn't all that difficult to separate individuals from the group as a whole, and we hardly noticed the conflict. The anti-Semitism came, after all, from people we trusted—parents and teachers and political heroes such as Goebbels and Hitler.

It was even easier when it came to believing in German superiority over other nationalities. A contempt for the rest of the world had been brewing since the end of World War I, and it was easy to believe that the countries we hated were inferior to us. We were, as a nation, exacting a sort of revenge; I'm sure it was for this purpose that, when accepting the surrender of France, Hitler arranged for the formalities to take place in the same railway car in which Germany had surrendered only a few decades earlier.

Although I had knowledge of the French from my encounters with the prisoners of war, I knew very little about the French as a people beyond the fact that the German Army had defeated them with almost no effort.

Of the Americans I as yet knew nothing.

The Russians were rumored to be brutal and prone to rape. Now, with the advance of the Red Army, Germany was fleeing to the West, hoping that an encounter with the Americans would prove less severe than one with the fabled cruelty of the Soviets.

Hitler's Iron Claw had lost its grip, and the hunters were being hunted.

After the initial strip search at Gestapo headquarters and the ensuing racial confusion, I was allowed a few hours' sleep. I awoke to cries of *"Scheisskopf!"* ("shithead") as a Gestapo officer kicked me in the ribs. I was dropped into a chair and the second interrogation began. A bright light was focused on my face. Two men asked me questions for what seemed like hours, periodically dumping me out of my chair and kicking me in the head or ribs. I wanted to tell them whatever they needed to hear to make them stop beating me, but I couldn't satisfy them no matter what I said. Realizing the futility of all of it I gave up and let them beat me.

When they were done, I was lying on the floor, limp as a wash rag, caked with my own blood. I was faintly aware of the stench of urine and excrement, and I realized that I had lost control of my bowels and bladder.

When I woke up, my entire body was swollen. Someone had stepped on my hand during the beating, and now my fingers had blown up and flushed with color like overripe fruit. I had a headache, and my face was swollen and crisscrossed with drying blood. A guard walked by and looked into the room, scanning the mess on the floor and walls.

"Get up and clean up this mess," he said.

I forced myself to my feet, wincing at the pain that shot down my side where I had been kicked too many times.

I looked around to find something to wipe up the blood and excrement, but there wasn't so much as a rag. I took off my shirt and wiped at a spot of spattered blood. The puddle dissipated into long streaks; the shirt was too saturated to absorb any more blood.

I got back onto my knees. Carefully, I wiped up the mess with my hands, sweeping it into one corner, trying to make it as neat as possible. When the guard returned, I stood in front of the puddle I'd created so that he wouldn't see what I'd been unable to get rid of, but he didn't seem to be concerned with the appearance of the room at all any more. He opened the door, grabbed me by the wrist, and marched me down the hall.

I was taken before another official, this time a man in civilian clothes. He asked the same questions I was asked earlier:

"What were you planning with the *Edelweisspiraten?* What is your connection to the French? Why did you take the shoes?"

I was afraid that this session would be a repeat performance of the previous day's interrogation, and I shrank in expectation of the beating.

To my surprise, the officer simply made a few notes and checks on an official-looking paper, filed it, then sent me shuffling to the washroom to clean myself.

At about 9 A.M. I was taken in a van to the city prison on the *Ulmenstrasse.* I had passed the prison before on my bike, on the way to the north-side swimming pool. My swimmer friends and I used to joke about the "Ulmer Heights Café," an entirely unattractive building that housed the local sleaze. It occurred to me as the prison doors clanged shut behind me that I was now a "café" patron.

There was a second strip search, during which we surrendered all of our belongings, exchanging our clothes and valuables for a prison uniform, a bar of soap, and a small towel. Following that, I was assigned a cell.

I looked around. The cell was a cube, about ten feet on either side and ten feet tall. The floor was polished concrete. There was no running water. On the one shelf in the room was a ceramic pot, which I correctly guessed was the toilet. Next to the pot was a rag, which I was later told to use to keep the cell spotlessly clean. There was a ceramic water jug, which I could refill periodically when I was allowed out of the cell to clean the pot. For furniture I had only a wooden stool and a small bed that hung from the wall on hinges. I was given one blanket, which I was instructed to fold neatly every day for inspection. My light came from a small lamp hanging from the ceiling. It was an older contraption, which could be raised or lowered and was counterbalanced with a ball filled with lead pellets.

At noon, a guard opened the door. I stood in the corner, unsure of what to say or do. He stared at me disinterestedly for a moment, then closed the door and locked it.

I had missed lunch. After that I always made an effort to stay sharp and aware of everything that was going on around me.

I learned that everything was very systematic in the prison, and that failure to comply with the regular order of things usually resulted in a missed meal, a beating, or a visit to solitary confinement.

When lunch was served, I was expected to stand ready to receive a bowl of soup when a guard showed up at my door. A trustee would accompany the guard and serve the broth.

In the evening it was the same scenario. A guard opened the door, stood at attention, and another prisoner handed me a thick slice of bread. The routine was so regimented that I could follow it without thought. When I began to grow hungry in the middle of the day, my body would automatically register that it was time for lunch and I would stand ready in my cell.

Things that at first seemed like a welcome departure from the tedium eventually blended into the drab background. My cell neighbor, for example, was either mentally disturbed or a fine actor, but far from amusing either way. He'd yell all day long, *"Liebe tante"* ("dear aunt"). He'd start off strong in the morning, shouting it like a holy proclamation. Gradually, though, he'd get hoarse, until by the end of the day his rasping voice would faintly drift into my cell, diminishing slowly into nothingness as he fell asleep. Every day was the same, *"LIEBE TANTE!"* in the morning to *"liebe . . . tante"* at night.

Eventually he was taken away after the guards found him eating his own feces.

Every day at 6:30 A.M. there was a great racket as the guards went from door to door opening cells. When my door opened I was ready with the ceramic toilet in my hands. I followed the other prisoners in a line to a giant hole where we'd empty the pots, then rinse them under a shared faucet. Then we were ordered to take a seat on a row of flushing toilets to do our business. At first, that gave me a welcome opportunity to exchange a few words with fellow prisoners, but after a few weeks I realized that I'd exhausted the topics of conversation, since nothing worth discussing ever seemed to pop up.

I was given a couple of different work assignments, but in each of them I was basically doing the job of a machine—actions repeated unthinkingly over and over until I was told to stop.

It wasn't the food that made life in prison hard for me, it was the idea of living in a cage.

I was bored.

To keep my mind occupied I dreamed up plots of escape. I thought constantly about getting out.

On my third day in prison my cell was inspected by a guard who lived in my part of town. It was obvious that he didn't like me much—he probably felt that I had shamed the neighborhood. He found a few old drops of sticky blood on the floor that had been left there by the room's previous occupant.

He went into a rage, screaming, *"Du Schwein, Du nicht-snutziger Scheisskerl, Dir werde ich's zeigen!"* ("You pig, you good-for-nothing piece of shit, I'll show you").

He ordered me to empty my pot on the floor and told

me that I had better have the room spotless by the next day. I was too terrified to object.

He left and locked the door behind him, leaving me alone with the stinking mess on the floor. I stared at the spot where he had stood, wishing that he would come back. I was ready for a fight. I opened my fists and closed them again, wanting badly to feel the heavy contact of a fistfight.

The door stared back at me, oblivious. I picked up my rag and began to scrub.

In my early days in prison I examined the prospects of several avenues of escape. I figured that, if I got sick, they would transfer me to a hospital, where I would have a better chance of sneaking out.

Starving myself was one possibility, but I wanted something that would produce results more quickly.

I was sitting on my bed and thinking when my eyes focused on the little counterbalance on my lamp. I got up and took a look inside. The lead pellet weights that balanced the lamp were smaller than marbles—not a hard pill to swallow.

I put one in my mouth, rolled it around for a minute, then swallowed. I could feel it sliding slowly down the back of my throat. When I couldn't feel it anymore, I ate another. Lead was poison, and I was sure that I'd be in a hospital in no time.

Unfortunately, I didn't get sick. I discovered the pellets in my ceramic toilette—they'd gone in one end and out the other. ·

I had to try something else.

My options were pretty limited—it wasn't as if I had any really nasty chemicals to drink or contagious friends to hang around with. I decided to stay on my lead diet. To augment this, I discovered some rusty nails in the corner of my cell.

I picked up a few of the nails and inspected them. They were about two inches long, of a medium thickness and completely covered in rust. Most of them were bent.

I put one in my mouth. I had developed a little bravery at swallowing things after my successes with the lead pellets. I took a deep breath, flooded my mouth with saliva, and swallowed. The nail was pinched tight in the back of my mouth, and it stayed put. I tried again . . . nothing.

I kept trying until I'd swallowed three nails; the taste of rust and iron lingered in my mouth for hours.

After a bit of discomfort with the next day's use of the toilet, I realized that the nails, too, were passing through me.

I had to swallow something bigger.

I carefully chipped a hefty chunk of ceramic off of my toilet pot by knocking it against the floor.

The difficulty I had in eating the piece of ceramic was only surpassed by the pain it gave me to pass it a few days later. I was, however, as healthy as anyone else throughout the entire experience.

I came to the realization that the combined efforts of my digestive and excretory systems would foil any attempt I made at eating my way into the hospital, so I resolved to take a different route.

I moved my stool to the center of the cell, away from the obstructions of walls and the bed. I stood on it.

I let myself fall.

Just before I hit the ground, the instinct of self-preservation forced me to throw my arms out and catch myself.

I tried again, failed, tried again, and succeeded.

I fell sharply on my head, saw a brilliant flash of white, then passed out. I awoke a few hours later with a throbbing headache, surrounded by a sticky puddle of blood about six inches in diameter. My hair was stuck to my face. It took me a few minutes to figure out where I was and what had happened.

I was still in my cell; no one had noticed.

There wasn't any serious damage—nothing that would get me into a hospital, anyway, so I had no choice but to clean up the blood before someone noticed it and realized what I'd been trying to do. It seemed that my only remaining option was to stop eating altogether.

After about ten days without food I collapsed while sewing buttons onto military uniforms during the daily work routine. Instead of being taken to the hospital, I received a severe beating. The guards insisted that it was the best way to get some good sense into me.

On April 12 I had my day in court.

Although my father had managed to hire two lawyers, there was little that could be said on my behalf. In Germany the burden of proof fell with the defendant, that is to say, you were guilty until proven innocent. (And I was, after all, guilty.)

The *Staatsanwalt* (prosecuting attorney) read the charges:

"Looting, sabotage, clandestine contacts and fraternization with the enemy, unlawful actions against the Hitler Youth, destruction of Hitler Youth–owned property."

He demanded the death penalty.

I had expected this, since the death penalty was mandatory in looting convictions (the supplemental charges were just extras, as far as the prosecution was concerned), but I doubted that I'd actually get much more than a slap on the wrist. All I did was take some shoes that were lying in the street (all lefties for God's sake!)—they wouldn't kill a sixteen-year-old over that. I'd probably have to listen to a speech about respecting the property of others, and then I'd be sent home to father, which was easily the harshest punishment I could fathom at the time.

My family did not share my confidence. My mother sobbed from the moment I entered the courtroom. She let out a loud wail as the prosecutor finished his introduction.

"This is not the last word," my lawyers said. One of them patted me on the shoulder.

The judge retired to his chambers, only to return after ten minutes with a verdict. I was sentenced to a minimum of one year and a maximum of four years in prison.

The judge explained, "the lighter sentence is being awarded in light of the young man's athletic contributions," and, since what I had done was not technically looting, "the death penalty is not warranted."

I could be released from prison to join the Armed Forces after one year of good behavior.

Only much later did I learn that my mother had visited the judge and pleaded with him to reconsider his decision. After making her wait three hours, the judge dismissed her begging in a few minutes. "Relax," he said, "it's not so bad. He'll be out in a year. You should be thankful that he's not being sent to a concentration camp with the *Judengesindel.*" His dirty word, "Jew rabble," made it clear that he would not have been so lenient if I had been a Jew.

Two weeks before being arrested I had sent in an application for voluntary service in the navy. During my time with the Hitler Youth, I had been trained as an underwater demolition expert, commonly known as a "frogman." I was only sixteen, and the regulations at that time required that anyone joining the service voluntarily needed to be at least seventeen. I lied, forging my father's signature to do so.

Five weeks later, three weeks after my arrest, orders

arrived from navy headquarters to present myself at their office in Wilhelmshafen. Under the circumstances, I had to surrender the appointment.

I often wonder what life would have been like in the German Navy. No doubt I would have been successful at the technical aspects of it; I was a good swimmer and I certainly wasn't afraid to take risks. However, in retrospect, I think I might have had a hard time with the rules and regulations of the Nazi military.

The more time I spent in prison, the less I was able to conform.

A few weeks after my trial I was transferred to Cologne, to the Klingelpuetz Prison, where I stayed for five days.

There were no showers in Klingelpuetz. To accompany the red bedbugs I discovered in my mattress, a colony of lice had established itself in my blanket. From the window in my cell I could look down into the courtyard. Apparently, executions were carried out there on a daily basis. Every day, in the afternoon, I was removed from my cell and made to wait until the executions were over before I could return. They wanted to keep the details a secret.

Though I couldn't see what was going on, I could hear the bell that signaled each prisoner's death. In my mind, I could picture it: the prisoner, blindfolded, being led out to the block by a leash, which served as a means of keeping him still until the bell rang and the executioner brought down his ax, removing permanently any need for a constraint.

Solitary Confinement

After five days, I joined a large group of prisoners who were being transferred to Koblenz. The prisoners were put in a train car with bars over all the windows, but I noticed a small window in the bathroom that didn't have any bars.

When we were about to cross the Rhine, I excused myself and made a second trip to the bathroom. Through the window I could see the river far below, and I knew that I could survive the currents if I could make the jump. Unfortunately, the tangle of steel pillars that supported the bridge would make jumping equal to suicide. I wanted to escape, but I also wanted to live. So I was stuck with prison.

Koblenz was a temporary detention unit—something like a military barracks. I was there for only three days before I was transferred with three other prisoners to Butzbach. From Butzbach I was moved to the *Jugendstrafanstalt,* a youth penal institution in Rockenberg.

Before the war, there had been only two basic types of prisons—the *Zuchthaus* for prisoners convicted of severe crimes, and the *Gefaengnis* for everyone else. Wartime innovation brought about a new variety of correctional facilities. In addition to institutions like my own, Germany also introduced the *Straflager*, which were penal camps, and the *Konzentrationslager* (KZ), which were concentration camps.

On the way to Rockenberg I was on the lookout for a chance to make a run for it. I kept my eye on the guard, waiting for him to lapse into momentary distraction. He'd look away for a moment, spotting a pretty girl or a passing motorist, and I would tense up, readying myself. Just as I would be about to cut down an alley or through a crowd, he'd refresh his attention on me.

He chuckled, "Don't even think about it. Don't give me a reason to put a bullet in you."

He caught me off guard with that remark, since I hadn't realized that he had been aware of my intentions. I didn't think he'd kill me, but I didn't want to test him.

"Things aren't so bad," he added. "At least you're not in Russia."

The prison was actually beautiful, if I limit my recollections to the architecture. The main office and its two satellite buildings were separated from the body of cells that made up the prison by a long road. Halfway down the road, equidistant from the main office and the prison building, was the prison kitchen. Next came the large courtyard in which we had our daily exercise. Surrounding everything was an enormous wall, giving the complex the appearance of a medieval city state. All of the structures were made of limestone two feet thick, adding to the ancient stature of the place and lending it the appearance of fortitude.

When I checked in I was given a uniform and a cell assignment. So that I wouldn't start off with a disadvantage, I began collecting whatever information I could about the daily routine.

Everyone had jobs, mostly manual labor for the war effort.

There were classes, mostly on "modern history," the defini-
tion of which, according to the German penal system, was the
history of Europe beginning with the rise of Hitler. I attended
a few of these classes, and found myself—despite my previous academic mishaps—at the top of my class.

Due to my superior education I received a work assignment as an assistant to the purchasing agent. The job was a
real gem. An elderly guard with a kind disposition, the purchasing agent was the type of man who made prison life a little
more bearable. I was even allowed to leave the prison with
him periodically to buy groceries and other items in town.

Already, then, I was making my way up the ranks of the
prison social system. Many prisoners envied those among us
who received "special treatment." With that envy came a de-
gree of contempt as well.

Most hated among the "special" prisoners were the kapos.
These men were selected by guards to act as supervisors,
usually following a long courtship on the part of the candi-
date. Typically, the animosity directed at the kapos by the
general prison population resulted in particularly cruel supervision—the rest of us would get more spiteful while the
kapos would get meaner.

The kapo who supervised my group had killed his parents.
His cell door was always open, he always got the best clothes
and food, and he enjoyed an amicable relationship with the
guards. It seemed a little strange to me that he would rank
higher than I in the system. No doubt the guards favored him
because they thought his crime was less severe than mine.

Still, I was happy with my assignment. I got along well with
my new boss and didn't have to be afraid of getting murdered by the other prisoners (the kapos enjoyed separate
quarters as a necessary precaution).

In fact, I was contented to the point that my ideas of

escaping had almost disappeared. I didn't want to disappoint and dishonor the purchasing agent by escaping while under his supervision. Still, though, I had higher aspirations than living in a cage for four years, and I kept my eyes open.

During my work I occasionally had the opportunity to inspect the smaller administrative buildings. In a small, empty room, I found an almost irresistible opportunity for escape. Over a period of years, the sandstone forming the window frame had crumbled away, and one of the bars could easily be removed. I decided that, sooner or later, that window would be my door to freedom.

Meanwhile, I received letters from home. The rules allowed us to send and receive one letter each month.

My mother was worried about my health. Assuring her that I was doing exceedingly well, I asked her not to be preoccupied. I promised to be home after a year. All incoming and outgoing letters were censored, so I wrote not only to console my mother but also to impress the censor favorably.

I didn't particularly miss my parents (I certainly didn't miss the fighting and the beatings), but I looked forward to hearing from them; it was a break from the tedium. Letters were a luxury, and personal visits were even better.

I was expecting a visit from my father. He had become something of an important figure in occupied France, working as a liaison officer for about 750 iron and steel factories in the north. Because of his expertise in the field, he'd been allowed by the German government to keep his relatively high-ranking position without becoming a member of the Nazi party. From what I understood of it, he had a number of connections in both France and Germany, friends who could help him out in a pinch.

My plan was to escape through the window and meet with my father, who would hide me in France. I described my plan to him on a small scrap of paper, which I planned to slip him during his visit. I told him where and when I would come out and where to wait for me with the car. It was a wonderful plan.

Unfortunately, things didn't happen quite the way I had hoped they would. A day before my father's visit, while I was trying to get out a key to get into the kitchen, the note fell out of my pocket. I didn't even notice it, but a nearby guard had seen me drop it, and consequently discovered my plans. I didn't suspect anything was wrong until an officer appeared at my cell door.

I was summoned to the warden's office on the third floor of the Administration Building. A guard ordered me to step into a painted white circle in the center of the room.

In front of me, sitting behind an abnormally large desk, abnormally far away, was the Warden, Dr. Zeugner.

"It is obvious that you do not appreciate the rather generous opportunity we have given you, Meyer," he said. "Personally, I thought you might have done very well here—I had even thought of recommending your early release so that you could join the Armed Forces," he continued. "Obviously, this is not the right course of action. Perhaps less comfortable accommodations will help bring back your sense of respect."

I wanted badly to sit down, but there were no chairs within the circle. I stared at the warden, a man who looked to me rather like a spider—his long, bony figure was complemented by a pair of rimless glasses perched on an aquiline nose.

"Twenty-eight days solitary confinement," he barked. "Take him away."

I was taken to one of the special cells reserved for "vacationers," a smaller, darker room isolated from the rest of the prison. There was a wooden bier, a jug of water, and a toilet. Everything that could have been used for suicide had been removed, which was probably a good idea in my case.

At about 6 A.M. I received my daily food ration. My time as a purchasing agent had taught me that the allotted proportion of bread for a day in solitary confinement was roughly two hundred grams, less than seven ounces. It was a special treat to get the heel of the loaf, which may have been a little larger.

I chewed the bread very slowly and tried to keep it in my mouth for a long time before swallowing it. While I was eating, I realized that I could hear myself chewing. In the absence of other noise and activity, it seemed loud.

Except for the guard coming with the food every morning, there was nothing for twenty-eight days. I contemplated suicide, thinking about throwing myself off the bed again or just not eating, but I always rejected the idea, reminding myself that twenty-eight days was not such a long time—less than a month.

I tried to keep my mind occupied by thinking about the people I knew. I thought about my parents, about friends, about my brother, about Elfriede. When I thought about Elfriede I thought about sex, and I was overcome by the sort of frustration that young men face all too often. I made a promise to God, swearing that, if he would protect me and help me to get out of the mess I was in, I'd give up masturbation permanently.

I tried to stay active by pacing back and forth in my cell. The rhythm of walking helped the time to pass. Sometimes, I would press my ear up against the wall and listen. I heard voices, real or imagined, moving about on the other side of the wall—prisoners more free than I.

Every time the door closed, however, after the guard had come and gone, and the heavy sliding locks clanked into place, I was reminded that I was completely alone. I began to imagine that even I didn't exist.

And when the door finally opened, not for a twenty-ninth ration of food but for my release, the light filtered in on what must have been a rather pitiful-looking young man. Thin and shivering, I was overcome with nausea as the light hit me and I realized that it was time to make a quantum shift back into the world of human associations.

I was joyous.

And disgusted.

From the cell I was taken, cramped and filthy, to the shower room.

The guard ordered me to undress. I stood underneath the showerhead, waiting for the hot water to stream over my body and for the thick steam to clear my nostrils and my mind.

The water crashed down on me, unbelievably cold. My muscles spasmed and I let out the smallest startled cry. My throat hurt when I made the sound, my first in days.

The guard laughed. "Cold water is good for the brain," he said. "It will make you forget those ideas of trying to escape."

He took me back to my old cell, which looked exactly the same, as if I'd only been gone a few hours.

I started work the next day.

I managed to get through most of the daily routine with only minor difficulty. The exercise program, however, was brutal for me in my weakened state. Formerly the most proficient of athletes in the prison, I found myself lagging behind even the most sluggish men.

"You act like my grandmother," a guard screamed at me. "Step forward and do fifty push-ups."

I tried, counting out the numbers as I went, only to be told that I had made a mistake when I reached thirty.

"Again. Louder this time," the guard said.

I started again, focusing my attention on the pebbles and cracks in the concrete under me, staring at them, studying them, living outside my body as it labored. I don't know how I reached fifty, but I was near collapsing by the time I was through.

I think that as the body deteriorates, so does the mind. One stops thinking logically—emotions take over. While I was struggling through my time on the exercise field, I spotted a metal pole that carried a light at the top. From the top of the pole, two heavy cables connected it to the other side of the wall—to freedom.

Again, the temptation was irresistible.

A few days later, after our early morning exercise, I decided to lag behind the group as we were being herded back inside. I got farther and farther away from the crowd until finally I was by myself. I made a run for the pole.

Large pocks and cracks ran the length of it, and using these as hand-holds I was able to shimmy up. I climbed with conviction, grabbing wildly as I worked my way toward the top, never letting my eyes leave the top of the wall which was my border to freedom.

There was a sharp snap, followed by a rush of air as I fell.

The bullet caught me in the left leg, near the ankle. The pain didn't hit me right away, but I was startled by the gunfire and frightened by the realization that I had been shot.

The fall knocked the wind out of me, but it wasn't enough to make me lose consciousness. I managed to get a look at my leg before the guards reached me.

Bullet wounds in the movies are clean, little red holes. In real life, a bullet hole is not so sterile. Blood was literally pouring out of my leg, leaking from the jagged tear that the bullet had traced across it.

The guards took a look at my leg, concluded that I probably wouldn't die, and abruptly hauled me off to solitary confinement. I passed out there, and was not up again until the following day, when I was revived by a guard.

Again I was taken to the third floor of the Administration Building, and again I found myself standing in the white-painted ring in front of the Spider Warden.

My leg had not been treated at all, and it was terribly difficult for me to stand up.

"Well then," began the warden, "it seems that your first vacation in solitary didn't do the trick. Perhaps the next twenty-eight days will finish the job."

I was hardly paying attention to him; I just wanted him to finish talking so that I could leave and find a place to sit down.

"Don't challenge my patience," he continued. "If you don't change your behavior, I'll be forced to think of a less pleasant solution. You're becoming quite a problem, Meyer, and I hate problems."

I was beginning to fade away; the room was getting darker.

"Do you think you will be able to change?" the warden asked.

I tried to move my head.

"Do you think you will be able to change?" he demanded, more insistent.

"Yes," I managed.

Then I fainted.

Two prisoners carried me on a stretcher from the warden's office to my cell in solitary. It was the same story as before: twenty-eight days, bread and water every day in the morning. I told myself that it would be easier this time, since I'd managed to survive it once before.

Under slightly different circumstances, this kind of positive thinking might have been able to hold up and get me through the ordeal, but as it was, with my still untreated leg throbbing and my chances of early release almost nil, it was hard to maintain a positive attitude.

I sat still most of the time, trying to avoid pain by keeping my leg immobile. I only got up to get my food every morning and to use the toilet on those rare occasions when it was necessary.

On the fifth day, as the door opened and I got up to receive my food, I was a bit confused. Usually, the guard opened the door and sent in a prisoner with my bread and water. This time, there was no prisoner, just an open door.

Slowly, I hobbled toward the door.

My eyes, unaccustomed to the light that was filtering in from the other side, could make out the silhouette of a guard standing there, propping the door open with one hand, staring at me.

Perhaps there has been a change of plan, I thought, perhaps they're going to let me out early. I took another step toward the door.

Suddenly, the guard hit me hard in the face.

I reeled backward as the door slammed shut.

There was no food that day.

Again, I contemplated suicide.

In the corner of the cell I found a few small shards of ceramic. The ceramic was not very sharp, and I had to use it as a saw to break the skin. My face contorted in a thick knot as I suppressed a scream. There was not much blood, however, and I was not able to cut the main vein. Eventually, all I ended up with were ugly scabs and scars.

I had to try something else.

Several flies had found their way into my cell. They pestered me almost constantly, landing on my leg wound and walking around, sending an annoying little tickle shooting through my entire body. Their pestilent nature had endeared them to rot, and my unattended bullet wound was irresistible. I swatted one, plastering his white, liquidy insides to the matted hair and clotted blood on my lower calf. I tried to clean myself, but then thought better of it. I'd found a resource.

I caught flies and other insects when I could, and placed these, along with dirt and my own excrement, into the wound on my leg. I rubbed the filth into the cut, peeling away as much of the scab as I could, hoping for an infection. If I got sick enough, I thought, they would pull me out of solitary and take me to the infirmary. I waited and prayed, but there was no infection.

The rest of my time in solitary was just as it had been the first time, except with more pain and more frustration.

When the time finally came for me to be released, I was elated.

The guard who let me out this time was not so brutal as the previous one, and even allowed me a few minutes of warm water in the shower. I was given clean clothes before I was returned to my regular cell, where I luxuriated the rest of the day in my bunk.

The same guard who had let me out of solitary showed up after my second day back in the general population, and escorted me to the infirmary. The nurse there applied some cream and bandaged the wound, telling me not to touch it so that it wouldn't get infected. I managed a bit of a smile.

I still had to attend morning exercises, but the guards seemed to soften up on me a little bit. The physical education officer, who was the man in charge of the field and everybody on it, encouraged me to try harder. He said it would help me recover.

"I'll settle for five push-ups," he said. "Come on, let's go."

I managed three, then stayed on the ground.

The officer ordered another prisoner to help me to my feet.

What sympathy I was shown didn't last very long. I still had a reputation as a troublemaker, and it was only a few days before things were back to the way they had been from the beginning. However, I resolved to stay out of trouble.

Given my previous record in escape attempts, I tried to put any thought of getting out at the very back of my mind. I went to work and to class, and I did my best to keep up with the others on the exercise field.

Deeply disturbed by the prison conditions and its adminis- tration, I found myself a quieter, more personal way of ex- pressing my feelings. An old atlas, borrowed from the prison library, offered a perfect canvas on which I could exercise my talent for drawing. The back side of each illustration was blank.

But what to draw?

The warden's spider face followed me everywhere, even in my restless sleep. I could have drawn an almost picture- perfect portrait, but the artist in me demanded some embellishment. I would create a cartoon masterpiece. I clearly identified the warden, complete with eight limbs, and added several likenesses of guards, with exaggerated facial features that made them appear comical to the point of grotesqueness.

I could hardly look at those drawings without bursting into laughter.

The guard who discovered the source of my joy was not so amused.

*   *   *

Back to the white circle.

"There seems to be no remedy for you," the spider said. "Perhaps you enjoy bread and water?"

This time, instead of fear or pain, I felt only anger. I wanted to jump across the room and grab the warden by the throat. I wanted to tell him that I refused to go back to solitary.

"Do you realize that you destroyed government property?" he continued. "Nobody can use this atlas any more."

I waited for the words that I knew were coming next.

"This is your last chance. Take him away."

Solitary.

I sat on the wooden planks in my cell and stared blankly into the darkness until my eyes felt pebbled and dry as the concrete floor.

My thoughts turned inward; I realized that I was seventeen, and that I might spend the rest of my youth in and out of solitary confinement.

I only got out of the cell once that month, for a visit to the infirmary for a checkup on my leg. The wound still hadn't healed, but there was no infection.

The nurse's eyes were kind.

"I'm sorry," she said, "I wish I could do more."

I didn't bother to count the days.

The same kind guard who had liberated me the second time brought me out of my third visit to solitary.

He allowed me a long time in the showers, turning on the warm water and then waiting patiently until I had had enough. As he handed me a clean uniform, he said, "Quit the foolishness—it won't get you out of here any faster. Try to behave and get out the proper way." He meant well, and I thanked him as he left me in my cell.

I sat on my bunk and cried for a long time. It was the first weeping I'd done since I'd been brought to prison.

Just as before, there was a period of kindness that followed my release from solitary—a sort of apology for the kind of cruelty that was all too common at the time.

A guard escorted me to the kitchen the next day, where I began my new work assignment peeling potatoes. I thought perhaps the friendly guard who had let me take my time in the shower had put in a good word for me to get me such a nice job.

On my second day in the kitchen, intense hunger compelled me to eat what must have been at least a pound of cooked potato peels. They made me very sick—I had to vomit and was given the day off.

My strength had dissipated greatly, probably due to atrophy. I tired easily and was not a very efficient worker.

One day, not too much later, I was ordered to report to the Warden's Office. I was scared, not knowing the reason for the call.

As I was standing there again, in that same white circle, I completely expected him to sentence me to another term in solitary confinement, although I had no idea why he would do so.

"I have decided that the best thing for you is some iron discipline," he said. "I cannot think of anything better than serving in the Armed Forces, so I have recommended you for the *Strafkommando*. You will receive orders within a week."

I had heard of the *Strafkommando*. The Nazi government, which was becoming desperate for manpower, had created a program for prisoners to serve as combat troops. Penal troops were usually sent into the worst places—front line operations that no one else wanted to risk. I'd only recently gotten over my suicidal mind frame, and the idea of charging headlong into a wall of Russian soldiers didn't appeal much to me.

After my meeting with the warden I joined the rest of the prisoners on the exercise field.

"What did he want?" one of the inmates asked me.

"He wants me to become cannon fodder," I replied.

My remark seemed to upset the other prisoner. He wanted badly to join the forces and had been rejected. He thought it insolent for anyone to gripe about the privilege of becoming cannon fodder.

Later that same day I found myself again in the white circle facing the spider.

"Did you say that you did not want to join the army?" he asked coldly.

I realized that my situation was very grave. I had made the remark earlier in a casual way and had no idea that I would be reported. I hadn't realized it at the time, but I had committed treason.

I tried to explain, "I just meant that, since I am not in good shape at the moment, I would like to have more time to rest before joining the army."

Spider didn't buy it.

"Get him out of my sight," he said, and I was marched to my cell.

The following day a guard appeared at my cell door.

"Get ready for transport," he said. "You'll be on your way to Sachsenhausen in the morning."

The Holy Trinity and
the Blood Brothers

It was March—a beautiful, clear, winter morning, the sun rising to watch as I was taken through the gates, which opened to the surrounding hillsides, into the back of a truck that was spewing black smoke, thick as pitch.

I was taken a relatively short distance to Frankfurt Railroad Station. Other prisoners arrived and waited with me on the platform.

The train rolled in, a loud black monster. Iron bars secured the windows of the cars reserved for prisoners.

"Everybody aboard. Take the first seat available," someone ordered.

I sat down in one of the wooden seats in a relatively empty car. The mass herds of prisoners had long since been rounded up and shipped off; there were only four of us in one compartment.

"Political?" the prisoner opposite me asked.

"*Ja*," I replied, not in much of a mood for conversation.

There was silence for a few minutes, each of us quietly mesmerized by the clatter of wheels and the rhythmic swagger of the car.

"Jude," the man said of himself.

I looked briefly at the yellow Star of David sewn into his clothing before letting my gaze settle on the man himself.

"Ja, Jude," I agreed, finding nothing to hate in this man who did not resemble me, "we are the same."

"Ja," said a third prisoner, speaking for the first time, "the Holy Trinity." He leaned forward in his seat, his frozen breath circling in a halo over his head, "and we will all die on the cross."

He was older. His scarred hands revealed him to be a man who had labored his whole life. He folded them behind his head, leaned back, and started humming a tune that was lost in the noise of the train.

The Jew and I placed our hands inside our sleeves and tried to shut out the cold.

I stared at the fourth man, who as yet had said nothing.

"Homosexual," the Jew whispered to me.

We traveled all day and through the night. The train was kept dark as a precaution against air attack.

I stared out the window in the twilight. The war had been going on for five years. Most of the houses in the countryside were abandoned, snow drifting as high as the eaves. The dogs that used to bark from the ends of chains were gone—the chains now lying forgotten somewhere under the snow to be a springtime reminder of a time past. Trucks sat rusting in driveways or on the sides of seldom-used roads. What traffic I saw was military, soldiers going or coming and, more often, transports for prisoners like us.

We received a ration of bread and some soup, served in aluminum containers and collected by a prisoner when we had finished eating. I managed to sleep, my chin digging a hole in my bony chest.

I was jarred out of sleep when the train came to an abrupt halt.

"Get ready, stand in line, follow orders!" the guards shouted as we got off the train. We had arrived in Berlin.

We waited for about half an hour, standing in relatively neat groupings until the second, smaller train arrived. Civilians in the station gawked at us awkwardly, probably wondering what we had done. Most tried to keep a safe distance.

The second train was to take us as far as the infamous Sachsenhausen Concentration Camp. I went back to sleep.

A few hours later, I opened my eyes when I felt an unexpected tinge of warmth. Searchlights.

"Hopp, hopp, dalli, dalli schnell, los, raus mit Euch!"
The SS guards were herding us out again, car by car.

We managed to arrange ourselves and come to attention. A young guard with a prominent jaw stepped forward and started prodding us with the butt of his gun, like a butcher checking the tenderness of his meat.

The gun found the Star of David on my companion's outfit and nuzzled him out of line and into the grip of two soldiers who escorted him off into the darkness.

The older man who had been talking to me on the train was again standing at my side, having stayed with me throughout the journey.

The guard reached me first and had his pistol jammed into my belly when the other prisoner said something I didn't quite catch, but that obviously offended the guard.

The inspecting soldier looked at me for a fraction of a second from underneath his braided cap, then turned his gaze to face the older man.

The sharp, punctuated report of his pistol shocked the hell out of me for a second; I thought I'd been shot. Then I realized that a trickle of blood was leaking from the other prisoner's chest.

He fell to the ground without making a sound.

"Too old, no respect," the guard said. "This is a work camp."

The butcher nodded to another guard, who grabbed me by the arm and led me in the opposite direction from the Jew, to a low building on the side of the parade ground.

They killed him, I thought. *Jesus Christ! They killed him right there, as soon as he got out of the train!*

I remembered what the man had said about crucifixion and I wondered what his name was, and if he had a family, and if they would ever know what had happened to him.

I was immediately ordered to fall in with a group of prisoners headed for the bathhouse. We stopped outside the doors to the building.

"Remove your clothes," a guard ordered.

I stripped along with the rest of the prisoners, feeling awkward removing my clothes outside in front of the guards.

They shaved my head, using a pair of clippers to remove everything but a little crown on top, which indicated that I was prone to make an escape attempt. The guards could keep a special lookout on potentially dangerous prisoners like me by looking for the special haircut. The system of marking us that way wasn't terribly effective, since our hair eventually thinned and fell out from malnourishment, but by that time the guards had gotten to know who was a troublemaker and who wasn't.

While they shaved me, I caught part of their conversation. Apparently, I wasn't going to stay here long; they planned on sending me to Ravensbrueck, a smaller camp, within forty-eight hours.

I was ordered to a barracks that served as a transit building. Prisoners of different nationalities were gathered there, waiting for orders to move to other camps. A man with a gray, bristly face approached me almost immediately.

"Want to buy some tobacco?"

His hand was cupped close to his body. He opened it slightly, revealing a half-dozen cigarette butts with the burned part cut off.

I had never been a heavy smoker, but for some reason I felt an overwhelming urge to smoke. I had nothing to barter except food.

"No thank you," I said.

I found myself regretting the decision. Would I ever get another chance to smoke a cigarette? My hands were shaking. Everyone was nervous here. Where were we going? What would happen next?

There was very little camaraderie. We did not participate in the camp's *Appell* nor in any other activity. We ate together but didn't talk much, choosing instead to stare into our turnip soup and think in silent fear. The prisoners formed small, loosely connected groups in accordance with their nationalities. I was one of the few Germans.

Early the next morning I was ordered to get ready. Along with two other prisoners I was taken to a waiting train. This was not a passenger train but a small locomotive with several cargo cars. It took only an hour to reach Fuerstenberg. From there we were loaded onto a small truck covered in canvas.

After only a few minutes we came to Ravensbrueck camp. I wondered why they hadn't ordered us to walk and decided that the guards must not have wanted the villagers to see us.

Our truck stopped and cut its engine.

I watched as two hands, each belonging to different bodies and each protected by massive woolen sleeves, reached into

the rear of the truck and dropped the tailgate. Voices somewhere behind the hands told us to step forward and get out.
I started to move forward with the others in my truck, but
we were too slow to appease the guards.

Grabbing us by the arms and legs, they hauled us out, leaving us in a giant human tangle in the dirt.

"Achtung!"

We came to attention. A guard ordered us to turn left and
marched us to the bathhouse.

A man behind me began weeping as he marched. We
were all terrified—we'd heard rumors that the bathhouses
served as death chambers.

A young woman guided us through the door to the bathhouse, and I felt my face turn scarlet as I tried to cover up in
front of her—the first woman I had seen up close in more
than a year. I was ashamed of my nakedness and how I
looked, and ashamed as well that I could still feel ashamed.

She led us into a large concrete room ringed with shower
heads and shut the door behind us.

There were no handles on the walls to turn the water on;
everything was controlled from the outside. I stood and
waited. There was a slight hiss, followed by the sound of air
moving through pipes, and suddenly the room was filled with
steam and scalding water.

It was the first shower that I had had in weeks, and the
water pounding down on me felt delicious. I closed my eyes
and tried to think of nothing, but somehow the image of
blood running down my dead companion's chest and the
water running down my own kept mingling. I tried not to
think about them burying his body somewhere while I
bathed.

I never again saw the woman who had led me into the
shower room, but I heard that some of the women prisoners

from the *Frauenlager*, the women's camp close to ours, per-
formed jobs like hers in our camp. I also heard that women
from the *Frauenlager* were frequently used in medical experi-
ments. I never learned the particulars.

"Das ist kein Luftkurort!" "This is not a health-resort!" a
Lithuanian guard screamed at me. "Move to the front!"

I shuffled out the door and encountered a large table covered with uniforms and shoes.

"To the left," I was ordered, and I steered myself around
the table.

Two prisoners attacked me with a bellows, puffing out
huge, suffocating clouds of flourlike pesticide. I was being de-
loused. The stuff clung to me, burning my skin and eyes and
making it nearly impossible to breathe. We'd have to tolerate
the nastiness of the insecticide until it wore off—having already had the obligatory first shower, another was not due
for quite some time.

The typical zebra-striped uniforms were not available. Instead, each prisoner was given a pair of black pants, a blouse-
type jacket, a hat, and a pair of wooden-soled shoes. Instead
of socks we were issued two pieces of light cloth, which we
could wrap around our feet like diapers.

Since I was a political prisoner rather than a Jew, I was not
tattooed. For identification purposes a number was sewn into
my uniforms, on the left sleeve and above the heart, next to a
crimson triangle, the insignia of a political prisoner. My number was particularly easy to memorize; I became 19445 in the
year 1944, when I was seventeen.

After I collected my uniform, a kapo directed me toward
my barracks. The camp was divided into blocks and barracks.
Several rows of fenced-in barracks took up the bulk of the

camp grounds, and these converged around an open plot called the *Appellplatz*. Each barracks was separated from the next by a washroom and a toilet, which was meant to be shared by several dozen men. A good distance beyond the farthest barracks, one could make out the offices and apartments of the SS.

I ended up in block three, where I joined more than four hundred other prisoners. Most of the prisoners in my barracks spent the majority of their time living in *Aussenlagern*, temporary satellite camps built near work sites. The kapo showed me my bunk, then told me that I was going to be part of a workforce outside the main camp, and that I would be evaluated after a certain period of time and possibly allowed to join Oskar Dirlewanger's penal SS brigade. The other prisoners explained to me later that the workforce was a mining team that stayed in an *Aussenlager* near the quarry. Besides me, there were several Russians, a few French, one Dutch, and no Jews. I was apparently the youngest.

Everyone seemed to be curious about the new prisoners. After being isolated for so long, almost anything new was of considerable interest to the inmates at Ravensbrueck. I was asked a lot of questions, about my crime, my family, my history, and especially about my money. I learned that prisoners were allowed to have and spend money to buy food and sanitary items in the canteen.

Early in the morning on my second day in the concentration camp, we were assembled for roll call on the *Appellplatz*. We were organized by number, the kapos channeling us into the right rows. Once everyone was accounted for, we waited and listened to some instructions over the loudspeaker. Then we were divided into different groups and herded off, mostly to trucks destined for the various temporary camps.

My group arrived at the quarry camp after a few hours of driving, and I had managed to gather a little information about my new home on the way.

The temporary camp, like just about everything else at that time, was organized by nationality—each had a separate section in the living quarters and a separate work area in the quarry. Russians had the unpleasant task of mining the bottom third of the quarry, where stray dogs and some of the smaller prisoners had been known to disappear; French prisoners took the middle section; we Germans were responsible for the top.

The *pensum* system was explained to me in more than clear terms: if you want to eat, you had better get your twelve lorries. Rocks were life. Failure was a cycle that fed itself. If you missed your *pensum* and didn't eat, you would be weaker the next day and miss your *pensum* again, and so on until you died.

I was less daunted by the *pensum* than some of the other prisoners; they weren't as young as I was, and nonstop rock mining was a real tax on their endurance.

I didn't receive very much instruction from the kapos or the guards, but another prisoner took the time to teach me how to find a vein, where to strike it with the pickax, and how to remove the pieces that were knocked loose.

Everything about camp life I learned from those who would teach me or those I could observe. There were certain tricks to survival, certain ways of dealing with things that made them easier.

Cooperation was a necessity, but among most prisoners there wasn't a sense of brotherhood. Concentration camps are not a good place to develop friendships. I talked to people from time to time, and some people tried to help me out a little since I was so young, but most prisoners were too concerned with survival to worry much about anyone else.

Still, I was glad for the scraps of conversation and advice I received in my first days. My trips to solitary confinement at Rockenberg had taught me the importance of human inter-action, at any level.

At lunch one day during my first week at the quarry, someone had approached me and said, "eat it again."

I learned to eat like a mother bird with her babies.

Sitting down for lunch, I'd take a bite of heavy brown bread, then a sip of lukewarm cabbage soup. After chewing slowly and bathing my mouth with the remote flavor and warmth, I'd swallow.

Almost instantly, I would bring the food back up.

Swallow again.

Repeat.

The benefits of regurgitation were remarkable. The food was actually warmer the second time through. I knew that there was no nutritional advantage, but psychologically it worked. We quieted the protests of our empty stomachs by tricking our bodies into thinking that we had eaten twice as much.

We grew comfortable with vomiting. Lunch time in camp was a privilege to be mined for all its worth. The half hour that was allotted to us daily was stretched to its maximum, every man making a deliberate effort to make himself as comfortable as possible. We were several hundred men, each weighing less than one hundred pounds, sitting on our laurels and vomiting repeatedly, desperately comfortable.

Unfortunately, the habit of re-eating my food became so automatic that I couldn't control it. For years I would find myself eating with friends or important acquaintances and suddenly realize that the food I'd just swallowed had returned to my mouth.

Sleep at the temporary camp came readily because we were all exhausted by the work. Food there consisted of a watery broth with some bits of turnips in it and a few pieces of bread. When it came time for our bimonthly visit to the main camp, I was delighted by the opportunity to get a break from the harsh conditions of the quarry. It didn't really occur to me that I was looking forward to returning to a concentration camp.

The periodic visits gave prisoners the opportunity to get clean clothes, apply for a visit to the infirmary, and send and receive mail. I was still forbidden to send or receive letters, however, and consequently my parents still hadn't been informed of my transfer to Ravensbrueck. Dear mother was still under the impression that I was safely tucked away in prison.

For the first time in a month, I had enough of a break between working and sleeping to collect my thoughts. I sat on my bunk in the barracks and realized that the will to survive had started to trickle back into me.

I looked at the men huddled in the opposite end of the barracks, vying for the closest spots around the tiny fire. They were wrestling over a few inches of territory, a few degrees of warmth to claim as their own.

I didn't want to die here, where no one would notice.

The respect for life in general that we usually take for granted had vanished, replaced instead by instincts of self-preservation. No one cared if other people died, so long as the self kept going, kept breathing in the known world, as miserable as it was, because the bite of the bullet on *der letzte Gang* (the last walk) might bring another quarry, where the rocks are larger and the meals smaller. People weren't afraid of death; death was part of the scenery. People were afraid of dying.

Personally, however, I was content. I didn't want to be here, but it was better than a solitary cell. I was so intent on living, so consumed with the belief that I would get out and be free again, that the thought of dying seemed almost hypothetical.

Though friendships in the camp were rare, I tried to talk to other prisoners when I got the chance. Most seemed willing to have a conversation, though usually not a very personal one; few seemed comfortable sharing sincere feelings. Of course, there were some exceptions.

I met a man from Saxony with a thick, almost comical accent, and the two of us talked for quite some time about the state of affairs in the camp and in the world around us. People called him Confucius in response to his philosophical musings. I saw him whenever I got the chance, and became one of nine prisoners who formed a sort of "inner circle" that listened to his theories and beliefs.

One day, while I was "home" for a weekend at the barracks, Confucius took on a very grave demeanor. I was sharing the sort of conversation with him that is filled with very long, heavy silences that carry more meaning in their ambiguity than words could in their clarity.

I knew there was something important he wanted to tell me.

He motioned for me to come close.

"I am dying," he said.

"You will not die," I said. "We will be free soon."

Silence again.

The other members of the circle had been gathering

throughout the day, and we were all present by evening. In our emaciated state, we must have looked like true ascetics.

Confucius had made a small blade out of a tin can, and he used it then to carve a design into one of the wooden posts that supported the barracks. It looked somewhat like a star, with three vertical lines and one shortly interrupted horizontal line. He explained that the three lines pointing up represented life, and that the line that intersected them was death. Though death passed through life, life continued.

"If we die," he said, "we die so that the next generation may continue; death will not come without purpose."

We protested that we would not die, that we would be liberated. We had heard rumors of the German defeats and the approach of the Russians, and we were all hoping to be set free soon.

Confucius persisted.

"We are brothers," he said. "We have lived together, we have suffered together, we will die together. Let us mix our blood in the way brothers have done throughout the ages."

He laid the jagged tin blade against his flesh and cut the starlike design into his forearm, then did the same to each of us. We pressed the cuts together and let the blood mix, becoming brothers.

Confucius died three days later.

Of those blood brothers, I am the only one left.

Will Today Be the Day?

After Confucius' death, I became intensely aware of the trials of survival that were playing out before me. Watching men regurgitate their food to kill their hunger pangs, watching the cycle of fatigue and hunger that started with a missed *pensum* and ended with death, I realized that life was budgeted here, calculated and parceled out into units of days and hours and meals.

Death was a measure of life, as well. There were no days, only the coming and going of people. Yesterday the bunk below me was occupied. Today it is empty.

I heard rumors, knowing that they were true, about prisoners in the remote parts of the quarry who had attacked a fallen worker with whatever sharp objects they could find, torn his warm liver out, and eaten it. Cannibalism was the secret to survival for some of the more desperate people in the camp; it was an experiment in Darwinism, a horrible and immediate example of the survival of the fittest.

It was a desperate time, and people were being forced to

be a little less than human to stay breathing. Those who couldn't compromise their dignity usually died.

I took a risk.

While my body was growing more and more accustomed to my surroundings, I tried to keep my mind alert, to assert to myself that what I was seeing had not always been, would not always be, and was not normal.

Everything was so surreal. Besides the simple inhumanity of the camp, there was a cultural disjunction that resulted from the throwing together of people, the herding and gathering and the cohabitation forced upon prisoners who came from different homes in different lands. New prisoners arrived daily, and the barracks was quickly filled beyond capacity. The new prisoners were from different ethnic and religious groups, and spoke different languages. Coexistence was only possible because it was necessary to survive; the instinct of self-preservation transcends the barriers of race and religion.

Some of the new prisoners spoke German or French, and from them I was able to gather some news from the outside. It was rumored that the war was coming to an end. It was 1945, and the Nazis were running out of manpower. Earlier in the year, Soviet prisoners were recruited to fight for Germany under General Andrei Vlassov. Some of the younger guards at the camp had been shipped off to join the war effort, being replaced by invalids. I was afraid that I'd soon be forced to fight for Oskar Dirlewanger in the penal brigade.

I began to wonder about Confucius. Had he been right? Would we all die before this war was over?

"Tomorrow will be better," I told myself.

But tomorrow was not better.

The fatigue I had been experiencing for the past few days abruptly abdicated to pain. My chest and ribs began to ache and I was gripped by the sensation of needles sticking into me, just above my stomach. Working was an enormous punishment.

I shared my feelings with Ivan, a German-speaking Russian prisoner with whom I had become familiar.

"You know what happens to sick prisoners," he warned.

Others reasserted the importance that I keep my illness a secret. I knew they were right.

When it came time to visit the main camp, I was looking forward to getting a break from work. After roll call, I tried to get some rest, but the pain kept me from sleeping. Sitting there, awake and miserable on my bunk, I suddenly sat up, needing to vomit. I went to the toilet and waited, sitting on the wooden frame over the commode hole. Due to the sub-zero weather and near absence of food passing through our guts, I was alone.

Blood began to drip from my nose.

The droplets fell and plopped onto the floor, blending with the concrete and frost. The blood kept coming, tapping out a largo rhythm and puddling into scarlet blotches barely visible in the dim light.

I sat on the splintered seat with my head in my hands, fascinated by the blood. I stared at the growing puddles and my eyes began to unfocus. There was a dizziness as the floor began to sway, but there was nothing alarming about it. Everything was growing darker.

A floodgate was opened somewhere in my head and the trickle of blood turned into an unbroken stream. I tried to stand up, but quickly lost balance and fell to the floor.

"I am dying," I said to myself. "I am dying."

It's interesting for me to think about how preoccupied I had been with the here and now. When I was miserable in life, I thought of nothing but death, and when I was faced with the misery of death, I thought of nothing but the need to stay alive. It's hard to make a rational decision when you're alive with pain; our base instincts tell us to get away, quit the pain and think later. Emotions take over.

"You are hurt, you are bleeding," cried one of the prisoners.

Many of the three-tiered bunks emptied as I stumbled back into the barracks. Everyone wanted to see.

The blood from my face had stained the front of my uniform and I had left a little crimson trail from the commode to the main room of the barracks. Some men quickly went to work cleaning up the mess so that no one would get into trouble.

One of the prisoners helped me out of my shirt, and a few others collected bits of kindling to start the stove. It was really a token gesture; such a tiny furnace was virtually useless in the middle of a German winter.

As I stood next to the little fire, the vertigo returned and I wanted desperately to get away from what seemed a spot of furious heat swimming in front of me. I fainted, striking my head on the edge of the stove as I fell.

Some of the prisoners must have carried me back to my bunk and cleaned me up so that I'd be ready for inspection. However, when I woke up the next morning, I knew that another day in the quarry would kill me.

It was Monday.

I asked the kapo for permission to go to the infirmary. He called me after roll-call and escorted me to the *Revier*.

"You may regret this," he said.

I didn't care. I knew that I'd die if I went to work, so I didn't have much to lose by talking to the doctor. I had to know the cause of the bleeding.

Also, I had already had the opportunity to spend three weeks in the infirmary, as a janitor. The regular prisoner had been sick, so I had been assigned to clean up the sanitary facilities there.

During my time as a janitor I had met Dr. Lucas, a native of Hamburg, then in his late forties. He was allowed to do little more than bandage open cuts and wounds, but he seemed intent on helping patients when he could. Most important, he seemed honest. When a patient was very sick, he told them so, breaking the news gently but not pretending that things were any better than they were.

I had found a couple of opportunities to speak with him. He told me that he had a son about my age in the German Navy. I told him about my own adventures in water sports, which seemed to warm his disposition toward me.

"What is that scar on your leg?" he had asked me.

I told him about being shot, and he took a look at the old wound to make sure that it was OK.

Here is a man who is still a man, I thought.

On this second examination, he inspected my forehead first, then asked about my nosebleed.

"Every time I breathe, my chest aches terribly," I explained. "Sometimes there's a sharp pain like needles in my lungs."

As if on cue, I coughed up blood for him to inspect.

It didn't take him long to reach a diagnosis.

"It's tuberculosis," he said rather calmly. "You are in very poor shape. You should not be working."

"Will I die?"

"I don't know. . . . I hope not."

I looked the doctor in the eyes, letting him see the vitality that was still hiding somewhere in my pupils.

"I don't feel so bad," I lied. "With a clean bill of health, I could keep working for quite some time."

For the doctor to agree to make a false report on my health would be a crime, and could land him in the quarry with the rest of us.

"I'll see what I can do," he said.

I looked questioningly at him, wondering what he meant by that.

"You are not going to be here for the rest of your days," he said.

I went back to work.

I later learned that the doctor died while attending German soldiers in a battle with the Russians.

I was able to do little actual work, and I was becoming panicky about meeting my *pensum*. Also, there was talk of an evacuation.

If the Russians really were coming, they were coming fast, and in order to stay ahead of them an evacuation would have to be even quicker. There were too many of us for the trains; we would have to march out in the dead of winter without food or rest. Already our barracks were overcrowded with men who had been evacuated from other camps, farther east, and their fatigued faces and racked bodies told us plainly enough what we could expect.

The door that leads to hope was closing in my mind, and I could see now only a slim chance for escaping with my life. I thought the kapos were beginning to suspect my illness. I tried to hide my eyes and pretend that I didn't notice them watching me, monitoring my performance. But it wouldn't last.

With the sudden influx of prisoners, Ravensbrueck had entered a period of mass liquidation. New gas ovens had been installed for the cremation of the dead, who were growing in rank almost hourly. This was not a death camp, but the authorities didn't hesitate to kill anyone who wasn't productive.

I decided to get out while I still had the strength to try. In my mind, a plan was materializing, creating a beginning and an end for an amorphous idea that depended almost entirely on the desperation of the times. I'd thought in the past of somehow getting out of the main camp and heading for nearby Lake Schwedt, where I might be able to swim to safety, but the idea was implausible at best; I had something else in mind now.

My uniform, a black synthetic outfit made from glass—not exactly fiberglass, but something like it—would pass as normal on the outside (minus the insignia and ID number), since even the civilians were wearing similar garments. Poverty had reduced them to it. My shirt would be difficult to alter, however, since the crimson triangle and my ID number were painted on. Some of the prisoners had shirts with patches, instead of paint, which could be ripped off with little difficulty. With one of those uniforms, I could become an instant civilian, although I looked like a scarecrow.

My visit to the infirmary kept me away from the quarry for a week, since I had to wait for the next transport. I decided that I could trade shirts with my friend Ivan when I returned to the *Aussenlager,* figuring that I would be able to keep the trade a secret from the guards by hiding the shirt under a jacket, a special treat I'd been issued to use in particularly cold weather.

My shoes were a bit odd, built with wooden soles and uppers of canvas which reached above the ankles. The laces not only kept them tight but also kept them from falling apart. They would pass, for a while at least.

Since most of the original guards had gone off to help the war effort, the watch had grown lax. The new guards were of several different nationalities, "drafted" from the various countries assimilated into the expanding Great German Reich.

They represented the Ukrainian SS, Polish SS, Rumanian SS, Hungarian SS, Lithuanian SS, etc. Though not as well trained as the German guards had been, these men were just as cruel, if not more so. They had gone the duration of the war in the shadow of their German counterparts, always remaining a little lower on the chain of command. Here was their chance to prove themselves, and they were responding like true zealots, though many had been badly wounded.

The invalids who guarded us knew that escape was not much of a reality: where would anyone go once they escaped? The camp was in a rural area, and most of the farmers had already left their homes and headed west to avoid the Russians. We were surrounded by miles and miles of cold, empty nothingness.

It was a perfect scenario.

The main camp had a fairly secure perimeter. There was an electric fence that surrounded the whole complex, with enough voltage running through it that you could hear it buzzing with energy several yards away. Although quite unnecessary, large, bushy coils of barbed wire adorned the top of the fence, raising its total height to more than twelve feet, the last two of which slanted inward, as if to stop someone from trying to vault over.

Most prisoners would never even think of trying to escape from that camp; the thought of getting near that fence was enough to make men shiver with fear. I remember one morning, as we were standing in formation for roll-call, a Lithuanian guard began teasing one of the prisoners. He grabbed the man's hat and tossed it against the fence.

"Go pick it up!" he ordered.

The prisoner's face was drawn taut in trepidation. He shook his head, cringing.

The guard brought his face within kissing distance of the prisoner.

"I said," he growled, "go pick it up!"

The prisoner remained perfectly still, except for a barely perceptible trembling in his hands and lips.

The guard started shouting profanities and kicking up dirt around the prisoner's shoes. He pulled out his gun and started prodding the man with the barrel, nudging him toward the fence.

The rest of the formation was ordered to march to work. As I stomped off, I could hear the guard behind me, beginning to beat the poor man. Apparently, the prisoner was more willing to accept a thrashing than to risk electrocution.

Yes, an attempt to escape from Ravensbrueck would be equal to suicide.

But an escape from the quarry? Here there was no fence; protecting the perimeter were only a few guards, and beyond that, forest.

My time away from the *Aussenlager* had gone fairly well for me. The work here was not nearly so hard as in the quarry, and since I was not Jewish and not a declared enemy of the Third Reich, the guards were not overtly mean to me. I was young, which was good in that it usually discouraged severe beatings, but bad in that it made me attractive to the few homosexuals in the camp. One guard in particular seemed to be giving me a little more attention than I felt comfortable with. I didn't like the way he looked at me, either. Fortunately, he was transferred not long after he noticed me.

But even in my relatively comfortable niche in the camp, I was restless. I knew that my only chance at escape would be from the quarry. My clean bill of health assured that I'd be returning to the *Aussenlager* with the next transport, and I waited and planned, determined to stay healthy long enough to die free.

My last journey to the quarry remains vivid in my memory. Somewhere in my belly I was filled with a confidence that came from knowing that I would succeed. My previous attempts to escape, back in prison, had been spontaneous—I had simply wanted out. Now I knew that there was nothing left for me but escape, and I knew that I'd either make it or be killed trying. Either way, I was going to be free of this place.

It was nearly dawn, time for the transport. We assembled near the exit gate, next to the parked trucks that would take us to the *Aussenlager*. A kapo counted off my group and we crowded into the vehicle bound for the quarry. I remembered that a few months earlier, we'd been packed tight in the truck bed. Now, with a few dead and the rest reduced by half their size, there was enough room to sit down or lean against the walls.

We waited quietly for a few minutes while the engine developed power. Due to the petroleum shortage, many of the diesel vehicles had been converted to steam power. There was no noise for a while except the hiss of the boiler, and then we started moving.

My view out the back of the truck was like looking down a tunnel. I watched as Ravensbrueck, with its twelve-foot-high electric fences and black crematorium smoke, disappeared into the horizon.

I tried to catch some sleep, but succeeded only in dozing off for a few minutes at a time before being awakened by the jostling ride or by the need to cough up some of the bloody mess that was filling my lungs. My last nap was cut short as the truck came to a stop and a train whistle released a long, angry scream.

All at once we piled out of the truck and onto a railway platform. I was grateful to trade my spot in the truck bed for one on the train, because the ride was much smoother. Someone remarked that he'd gladly volunteer to shovel coal if only he could stand near the boiler.

Our transport would be a shorter trip this time than it had been in the past. We'd often had to ride the trucks all the way to the *Aussenlager* when the trains weren't available. Usually, we'd have to change trains somewhere along the way, which often meant a long wait in between. Today, however, we made only one short stop on the twenty-mile trip, and we were allowed to remain huddled in the relative warmth of the cabin for the duration.

At about eight o'clock we arrived at the quarry camp, and we were put to work as soon as we'd gotten off the train. A shiver of anticipation ran the length of my body as I again noted the proximity of the quarry to the surrounding woods, and, miraculously, the absence of fences.

A kapo checked in with a supervisor and gave us our instructions for the day. Mine were always the same: digging rock and loading twelve mine cars. The only variable was the area I was assigned to work in, which was rotated daily. Most prisoners had the same assignment, but a few were given the tasks of tearing up and repositioning the rails for the lorries or carrying water and doing other odd jobs as needed.

My exit would be the perimeter of the quarry, which was patrolled by armed guards but was the fastest way to get to the forest. I intended to make my move when my work assignment returned me to the uppermost level, not today, but soon.

It was just after New Year's, 1945.

The day had started as usual, a bugle blast reminding

everyone to wake up at five o'clock. We had to be ready in a few minutes.

Carefully, we wrapped our feet with precious scraps of newspaper, or, for those of us who still had them, with the pieces of cloth we'd been issued on arrival. There was no need to change clothes—we had only one uniform, which we never took off. Following the kapo, we shuffled down a hallway and into the dining area. As we stood in line we could smell the steaming broth.

"Hey kapo," one of the men asked, "maybe we get cross-country today?"

"Cross-country" was a soup with an almost unrecognizable mixture of ingredients. From what I could tell, it consisted of potato, cabbage, rye, and grass. Mostly, though, it was water. We didn't use our spoons anymore; we just drank our meals out of the bowl.

Meals seemed thicker in the main camp—perhaps the SS thought they could fatten us up during our monthly visit.

Any scraps of meat that might have been in the soup sank to the bottom, and for this reason the trustees ate last. Our trustee gave the man who had asked about the soup a disinterested glance, then started moving with the rest of the line toward the servers. One prisoner ladled out each man's ration of broth, while another replenished the supply of bread as it was given out.

I sat down and started eating.

It was the same routine: sip, vomit, swallow, sip.

I watched Ivan, the Russian prisoner who had traded shirts with me. He was finishing his chess set.

A half-slice of heavy brown bread disappeared into his mouth, where he chewed it for a few seconds without swallowing. Then he spat the goo back into his hand, where he began to turn it over, shaping it. He rolled it between both hands, making an oblong little stick. This he flattened at either end, then carved at with his spoon. Once it dried, it would be a passable black queen.

Ivan loved chess.

After lunch, we were allowed five minutes to use the latrine.

"Going to give a try at the thunder beam again?" one prisoner asked me.

"Yes, Heinrich," I replied, "I ate so much I'll be sitting there all day."

The joke was as tired as we were, but it was important to try to keep a little humor in the barracks to help the time pass. The two of us dropped our pants, unbuttoned the seats of our long underwear, and sat carefully on the edge of the wooden plank we called "the thunder beam."

"I heard that you were here when the beam broke two months ago?" he asked.

I made a sour face. I remembered the incident all too well.

Heinrich was fishing for a good story, and asked, "How did it happen?"

There had been about fifteen of us on the beam. When the last man sat down, there was a loud cracking sound. The five of us in the middle never had a chance to react. Someone had sawed halfway through it, and the weight had caused it to collapse. A few men saved themselves with some quick acrobatics, but I ended up with about half a dozen others in a pile of shit that had been accumulating for God knows how long.

Another prisoner had joined Heinrich and me on the thunder beam, and he had started listening to my story. "Who did it?" he asked.

"The guard with the big ears. He was waiting just outside

the door, and when the beam broke, he ran in laughing so hard that he started crying and choking. We tried to get out, but the ground was so slick that most of us just fell down again, which amused the hell out of the guard."

Heinrich took a quick glance behind him. He didn't seem to think that it would be very funny.

"Then he started yelling at us," I continued. " 'You sons of bitches, you've got five minutes to get out and clean up!' The first man who made it out got a kick in the chest and tumbled right back in. That guard didn't stop laughing for an hour, yelling at us the whole time while he made us clean up the mess and replace the beam. I guess he got his kicks for the day."

"The pig," Heinrich murmured, testing the wood next to his bare bottom with a little slap of the hand.

The prisoner who had joined us was eager to hear more, but I didn't feel like talking about it any longer. Retelling the story made the feel of it come back again, in my hair and ears—all over me. And that stench. Having worked as a youngster with animals on Granduncle's farm—cattle, horses, pigs, just about everything—I can testify with unwavering certainty that nothing is as repulsive as human manure. Nothing.

We could hear the voices of the guards approaching the latrine area.

Time to go.

We tore off tiny scraps of the newspaper we'd stuffed into our long underwear and cleaned ourselves. *Das Reich* wasn't read much in camp, but it was great for insulation, toilet paper, cigarette paper, and even the occasional bandage.

The kapo began roll-call, then hollered out the cadence, "one-two, one-two, one-two . . ."

Everyone moved in perfect unison, latching on to this tidy semblance of order in the chaos of the camps.

Would today be the day?

I thought back to my first day in Ravensbrueck, just after my transfer in 1944, when I had been offered the choice between hard labor in the quarry and somewhat easier work in the base camp. The other prisoners had called me crazy (or stupid, in some cases) when I chose the quarry, but I had my reasons, even then. I knew that I'd have a better chance of escaping.

The kapo exchanged a few words with our escort guards, then called out, "right face, march!" And we turned and began walking in two columns toward the small road that led to the upper level of the quarry.

It was a lonely walk.

There was no talking, only snow crunching under our feet in a steady rhythm, to a march that had no flags, no salutes, no military music.

We stared at each other's backs or at the ground, concentrating on the cold in our unprotected hands and ears. Only one prisoner seemed to have an interest in the scenery.

Would today be the day?

I collected my only tool, a small, short-handled pick. Occasionally I was allowed to use a steel breaker bar, but not this time. As I pushed my lorry along its track, I stared out over the pit, about a half mile across and more than two hundred feet deep. Exposed to the damp, Baltic air, the temperatures in the quarry were always below zero at this time of year.

Today the cold brought with it a thick, gray fog that rolled in off the top tier and then sank to the bottom of the pit, hiding the freezing Russians at the bottom as they hacked their way through the rock. The mist seemed to exaggerate the sense of boundlessness—and hopelessness.

What if today *wasn't* the day?

"The *pensum!*" I blurted, breaking away from my daydreaming. I began scanning the rock walls frantically, searching for a large enough vein to get me started. A good, concentrated deposit, struck in just the right spot, could reduce the day's work by half. Otherwise, I'd work myself to death trying to search out smaller veins that wouldn't begin to fill a lorry. I can remember watching other prisoners who were two or three lorries short of their *pensum* frantically scurrying across their tier, praying to find a vein, as the workday neared its end. The same men could be seen a few days later, sitting idly and letting the hours dissolve without so much as one stroke of the pickax—they'd given up.

Fortunately, I'd never gotten to that stage.

After about half an hour of probing the beige-colored rock walls of the quarry, I found my vein, a long, winding gray streak. Using my pick as a lever, I pried at it wherever I could get purchase, tapping the blade lightly into place and then heaving against the handle.

A sharp crunch punctuated the little avalanche that erupted from the quarry wall as the large chunks of rock tumbled out. I stumbled backward, trying to avoid the landslide, but I was too slow. I caught a glancing blow on the calf from a fifty-pound rock. I knelt in the dirt and pulled up my pant leg, examining the already darkening bruise.

In my weakened condition, the proud purple blotch would be there for weeks before it healed, but that wasn't what I was worried about. Carefully, I checked to see if I'd broken the skin. Tolerance to infection in a concentration camp is nonexistent, and I'd seen small cuts kill a man before.

The skin was broken, but not badly. I had survived the cut on my forehead, and I would survive this as well. Back to work.

Limping slightly, I spent the next few hours loading lorries. My arms were too weak to manage rocks any bigger than twenty-five pounds, so some of the bigger chunks had to be broken down before I could load them. My back had long since lost the strength to let me do any real lifting, so I hoisted the larger rocks onto my thigh and then raised my knee until it was level with the lip of the lorry and I could push them in.

The faster I worked, the more I coughed.

I tried to pace myself.

I finished filling the first lorry, and pushed it to the end of the rail.

"Number 19445," I called, taking another car for the return trip.

"Jawohl," responded the kapo on duty. He recorded the lorry in a little notebook, deducting it from my *pensum*, then pulled a lever that sent it clattering over the edge of the tier, riding a cable down to the mill. Only a few prisoners worked in the mill—none from my group—so we never really learned how the rock was ground, but we could hear them working in there, their machinery groaning and hissing incessantly, starting about half an hour into the workday and continuing until after my group had left for dinner.

Walking back to my spot at the top of the quarry, I could see the lorries disappearing behind the corrugated steel walls of the mill as they entered via a large rectangular hole in its side. On the opposite end, a small train with open cars pulled away little mountains of the gray powder that was mixed with traces of our blood and sweat.

By four o'clock, I had filled my last lorry for the day. With no work to keep me moving and warm, I stood behind the loaded cart and tried to hide from the wind.

I attempted to look busy to appease the guards, but whenever they turned away I ducked behind a cleft in the wall, sliding to the ground and sitting. What a luxury! There were very few occasions when I'd been able to finish early enough to take a rest.

Of course, the cold put a damper on things. My hands suffered the worst. Callused and terribly chapped, they were almost constantly exposed during labor. Taking advantage of the break, I stuffed them into my pockets, pressing the palms against my thighs for extra warmth.

There was a dull but powerful ache in my ears that I knew was mild frostbite. I had no scarf or muffler, so I pulled my head into my shoulders as best I could, like a turtle hiding in its shell. The pain persisted, however, and my attempts to ignore it were becoming less and less effective. Finally, I covered my ears and cheeks with the palms of my hands in a futile attempt to exchange heat from one frozen slab of meat to another.

I had to keep moving or I was going to freeze to death.

I approached a guard.

"The outhouse sir," I said.

"*Ja*, pass," he responded, uninterested. It was a normal enough request.

I passed a few other guards on my way to the outhouse, but they could guess where I was headed and let me go unmolested.

Already exhausted by my work, I walked slowly, with great effort. Coughing spasms racked my body, and my lips and chin were soon coated with a slick layer of bloody spittle. Luckily, the camp was only a little above sea level; thinner mountain air would have made me pass out.

When I reached the outhouse, I took a look behind me. There were only two opposing walls for the small building, so I had a good view of the guards and they could see me as well. Whoever had designed the thing must have wanted to make sure that someone could keep an eye on us in case we decided to escape through the conspicuous hole in the ground.

If anyone cared what we were doing in the outhouse, however, it wasn't apparent now. I was directly in the line of sight of at least two guards, but neither of them gave me so much as a passing glance while I was in there; neither one of them seemed interested in watching a prisoner defecate.

By the time I returned to my post and emptied that last lorry, it was five o'clock—quitting time. A steam whistle from the mill announced the end of the shift, and we assembled at the toolshed, returning our picks and trudging home, slowly descending to the camp. The sun reached the tops of the nearby pines, then slowly slid behind them, sending out shards of refracted light that brilliantly lit up the pit, tinting the beige rock walls with a mellow gold that outlined the long, broken shadows of the men who marched solemnly past, tired, cold, and hungry.

We went immediately to the dining area, where a kapo stood guard at the door to make sure that nobody got through who hadn't met their *pensum*. The unlucky ones were left outside the entrance and watched as the rest of us went through the line, while the one or two men who had been above quota were given a little extra for their efforts.

Almost without realizing it, I stared at the skeleton men who weren't allowed to eat. It should have been easy for me to sympathize with them—I had gone once or twice without food myself—but I just couldn't seem to understand the hunger in their eyes. I did a little self-examination.

I felt tired; that was nothing new.

Pain racked my whole body; understandable, I had tuberculosis.

I wasn't even remotely hungry. This was bad.

I got my food and sat down with it, trying to take a few sips of the broth. It tasted metallic; eating an entire ration of it would be like drinking a pot of cold coffee—it could be done, but not without a real effort. I looked around at my fellow prisoners, all of whom seemed to be content with the meal. Something was *wrong*.

I managed another few swallows of the soup, then gave up. Hiding a bit of my bread, I gave it to the prisoners who hadn't met the *pensum*.

I had seen men give away food before, and it was never a good sign.

Conversation died quickly on Monday evenings, most men too depressed at the thought of the week ahead to be very talkative. I collapsed facedown on my straw mattress, breathing in the remote grassy smell that was hidden under the stronger odor of my sweat-stained blanket. It was long before the eight o'clock lights went out, but nobody remained on their feet longer than they had to.

I was exhausted, but a buzzing in my brain that accompanied a dull headache kept me tossing and turning for a few hours. Beads of sweat formed on my forehead, and out of a desperation to escape the extreme discomfort of being awake, my body slipped into a harried half sleep, colored with images of the quarry, of the woods beyond, of flight.

A large Lithuanian guard was running after me, hand outstretched, grasping for a handhold on the back of my collar. I was able to stay only a few inches ahead of him, and the burning in my lungs and the pain of exertion was too much for me to keep going for long. I dodged a lorry that had been left blocking the path along the tier, nearly lost my balance, recovered. Glancing behind me, I could see the guard losing distance. Two prisoners pointed after me, trying to be as helpful as possible to the SS. The path split and I chose the high road, hoping to get up and out and into the forest. It was a short distance, but the uphill climb was slowing me down. Almost to the top, I was hit head-on by a jolt of fear as I heard dogs, barking and racing after me with animal speed and an instinct to kill. And through it all, someone was shouting "Number 19445! Number 19445! Return to your post immediately!"

When I awoke, my blanket was lying on the floor of the barracks, but I was covered in sweat. I coughed harshly and felt the now familiar taste of blood in my mouth. I swallowed hard, reasoning that it was better to keep blood inside the body than to let it out. It was still hours before dawn, and in the quiet of the night I had a chance to turn things over in my mind. The rusty taste lingering on my tongue was a reminder, like the tolling of a bell, that time was short. I had to get out. The moment would present itself, and I'd take it.

The resolve calmed me, and I went back to sleep.

Morning arrived like so many others: a whistle called us out of bed and into the breakfast lines, then there was the short and silent march to the quarry. Again, I had passed up my chance to eat, breakfast not sparking my appetite the way it always had in the past.

I spoke to my friend Heinrich as we checked out picks from the toolshed together in the morning.

As we turned and were about to head off to our respective stations, the short figure stopped and smiled at me.

"How are you today, Walter?" he asked.

"I'm fine, Uncle," I replied. It was a name that seemed to fit him.

He didn't know what I was planning, no one did, but the confidence in his eyes seemed to be wishing me well, as if he could guess that I was up to something important.

It was an average day, another twelve lorries and another meal earned, uneventful except for Heinrich's death. The news reached me in the late afternoon as I passed another prisoner on my way to the drop-off point. No one knew how it happened, but deaths were common and there wasn't much speculation. I was too tired to be upset.

That night there were no dreams, and I slept in peace.

On the third morning, with the soup served cold and the bread going stale, I was not alone in rejecting breakfast. As we left the dining area, we were greeted by a thick blanket of fog. Typical at this time of year, the fog lengthened the night by shutting out the feeble light of dawn, leaving us in a wet and chilling darkness.

We moved toward the toolshed, and I peered into the mist, spotting an occasional lantern or headlight in the distance, glowing strangely out of focus in the enveloping grayness. We collected our picks, but we couldn't start working because the terraces weren't equipped with artificial lighting. Someone behind me started mumbling, worrying about whether we'd have enough working time to meet the *pensum.*

The moisture magnified the cold weather, and we huddled into groups and shuffled around to stay warm. Visibility was low, and the only thing discernible for about a hundred feet was the silhouette of a guard with a rifle, haloed by the light coming from the supervisor's office.

We waited in silence for nearly an hour and eventually a few rays of sunlight filtered through the fog and provided enough light to work by.

"To your places; let's go, *hopp, hopp, los . . ."* ordered the kapo, useful and in a hurry once more. He had already assigned positions for the day, and my group was once again at the uppermost level.

We broke away from the main body of workers and

headed for our area on the top tier, feeling our way along the rock wall where vision was too obscured to see the path. A few stragglers fell behind the rest of us and were swallowed by the milky haze, lost from view.

I found my spot, got a lorry, and pushed it to the end of the track to start working. I looked for a vein, realizing as I did so that the fog would make it difficult to find the good deposits. You couldn't see anything up here.

Not even prisoners.

The dense air muffled the sounds of the picks chipping away at the rock and the cars clattering over tracks.

My heartbeat was throbbing in my ears.

This was it.

I sat down near my lorry and planned it out; this was not going to be another spontaneous escape attempt. I waited for about fifteen minutes, resting, thinking, and gathering my strength.

Standing, I took a moment to calm myself so that I wouldn't look suspicious, then headed for the outhouse.

My heart nearly stopped when I encountered a guard along the way. I asked permission. He waved me on.

The guards were mostly older men, vulnerable to the bad weather. When they should have been doubly vigilant, they were doubly lax, concentrating only on the cold and how much better they'd feel back in their quarters next to a fire.

The latrine sat only a few yards from the edge of the pit. On a clear day, I could have seen the barracks from there, about five hundred feet to my right. The forest was about the same distance to my left.

I pulled down my pants and sat on the little hole, trying to maintain the appearance of normalcy. I held my breath . . . no footsteps, only the thumping of my heart.

I pulled up my pants and stuck my head out the left opening. I might as well have stuck it into a bottle of etched glass; the cloud was sticking fast, thick as wool.

The first hundred yards of ground barely felt the touch of my wooden shoes. Adrenaline surged into every muscle as I tore my way through the cotton shroud. I dodged tree trunks coming into view only a fraction of a second before I was upon them, narrowly missing a few bad collisions. But they didn't seem like obstacles, they seemed a crowd of welcoming people, opening their arms and inviting me home, closing ranks behind me to conceal my flight.

I ran with an energy I should not have had, plunging wildly through the forest for what might have been a whole hour before coming to a clearing and stopping, chest heaving, eyes searching the fog for the guards that I knew must be in pursuit.

Silence.

I took a few steps forward, toward a part of the clearing that seemed to lead to a great gap in the trees, perhaps a large road . . .

My entire body jerked back in alarm.

I was at the lip of the quarry. I must have been circling the perimeter the whole time, probably on the verge of plunging over the edge more than once as I sprinted for freedom.

I felt a cry of anguish welling up in my throat, and only stifled it with a great force of effort. I was boiling over with frustration, but they hadn't seen me yet; I still had a chance.

I turned around and darted off again, this time wary of my bearings.

My senses were dancing with blurred images of hope and anxiety, making the run seem longer and more desperate than before. I lost the rush of energy with which I had begun my flight, and I stumbled in slow motion through the woods, gasping for breath as I was slapped in the face by boughs of pine and spruce. I tripped over small bushes, lost my shoe somewhere and didn't notice it until I'd left it far behind me. I leapt over broad gullies only to sprawl headlong into shallow, leafy depressions hidden by beds of pine needles.

At last, with my chest on fire and my mind swimming, the terrain leveled out. The fog grew lighter and disappeared with the trees. Ahead of me, in the center of some sort of pasture, I could make out the dark outline of a wooden shelter.

It was a hayrick—an open shed that farmers use to store alfalfa-hay in the winter.

I was getting dizzy and light-headed, and knew I had to stop. If anyone had caught me, I would have been incapable of resistance. I collapsed in the hay, spreading it over my body to give me a little insulation.

I just wanted a few moments' rest, a second to get warm and catch my breath before I started moving again. They'd be looking for me soon, and I had to put as much distance between myself and the quarry as possible. I'd catch my breath, and then I'd go.

I passed out.

Later that same day (or possibly the next), I awoke with a start. I opened my eyes and found myself staring into the face of a man I had never seen before. ·

"Don't be afraid," he said.

But I was.

A Taste of Freedom

The man who found me had the rough look of a country farmer. His hazel eyes were shaded by the floppy brim of a tattered hat and his face was adorned with thick, bushy eyebrows and a wide mustache that completely covered his upper lip. Kneeling next to me, he could read the terror in my eyes, and he spoke calmly to keep me from panicking.

"I know where you came from, and I'm going to help you," he said.

My heart continued to race, still wary of the stranger.

"I'm going to take you home with me," he said.

I looked carefully at him, gauging his words. The camps had given me confidence in reading people, and what I was hearing now seemed sincere. At any rate, I was in no condition to put up a fight.

I felt cold and reached to button my jacket. My hands were shaking and I stared down at them, trying to bring them under control. Between my groping fingers, I could see a faded outline where the red triangle and the white ID number over my heart had been. My hat was gone, I realized, and what was left of my blond fringe was totally visible. I was completely exposed.

The farmer rested a gentle hand on my shoulder. "I lost a son in Russia last year," he said. "He was your age."

With that, he helped me to my feet. My legs were virtually useless, so he held me up as he propelled me to his wagon, then lifted me gently over the side. He covered me with hay, letting me go back to sleep as the horses pulled us through the fields. Perhaps an hour later, under the bright midday sun, we arrived at the courtyard of a modest stone cottage. Hoisting me out of the wagon, he carried me in his arms to a bed inside, where he let me rest, wrapped in a fluffy down comforter.

A large iron cooking stove warmed the main room, and for the first time in months I had the experience of genuine heating. My bed was near the stove, and I watched the flames dancing behind the iron grill as the farmer nursed me and spoke to me in a monologue, trying to comfort me with friendly conversation. He bathed me, careful not to further damage the skin that had been bruised by work or worn away by rubbing against my bones. He shook his head in disbelief as he looked at my emaciated body, unable to understand how a human being could be so much reduced and still survive—it is one thing to pass a group of withered prisoners on the road or to see them in a photograph, but quite another to have one lying in your house, alive in a dead body.

I was offered a substantial soup, and when I refused it, I was forcibly fed, the farmer putting each spoonful to my mouth and leaving it there until I sipped some. He helped me to the toilet, then dressed me in clean clothes—his son's.

Throughout the experience I said nothing. Perhaps I was in shock, unable to speak for fear of disrupting my streak of good luck. My new friend was tolerant, though, and continued to share his thoughts with me. He talked to me while he tidied up the room, picking up the clothes on the floor.

"I am my own housekeeper now," he joked. "My wife left three days ago with the other women. We've heard that the Russians aren't far off, and there are rumors of rape and stories of soldiers killing babies when they won't stop cry-ing—I hope to God that it won't be as bad as that here."

Though I didn't know it at the time, the Russian troops had in some cases been encouraged by their leaders to be as brutal as possible. The Russian nationalist writer Ilya Ehren-berg once wrote, "Soldiers of the Red Army, the German women are yours." Her writings were sanctioned by the Soviet government.

My farmer friend scratched his bushy head. "They'll be looking for you everywhere by now," he said. "I plan to evacu-ate soon, so I can't keep you here for more than two days."

I was getting nervous.

"Don't worry," he said, seeing the fear creeping back into my eyes, "I have a plan. Every morning I carry the milk into town, where trucks from the cooperative take it to the dairy in the city—we aren't allowed to process it ourselves any-more; they were afraid we'd sell butter on the black market."

He paused for a moment, seeming to realize that his liveli-hood wouldn't amount to much within the next few days. He must have understood the futility of taking the milk to a town that would soon be swallowed up by a foreign power, for money that would soon be worthless in the impending crush between the Allied armies.

"Anyway," he continued, "you can ride the milk truck into the city, and from there you can take a train somewhere, per-haps Berlin or Cologne—"

"To Duesseldorf!" I blurted.

"Well, you *can* talk!" he said, smiling and chuckling a little.

"My home . . . my parents live there," I explained.

"Good," he replied.

He stared at me for a moment, probably wondering whether I was aware of the steady bombardment that had all but flattened the city.

"How long were you imprisoned?" he asked.

"Two years."

"How old are you?"

"Eighteen."

He shook his head.

"You'll see that a lot has changed since you were last home. Germany is not the same country any more." He stared absently into space for a few seconds, then disappeared and returned carrying a bundle of clothing. Unfolding it, he produced his son's uniform, with the markings of an infantry corporal.

"You won't need any papers," he told me. "Just tell anyone who asks that your entire unit was destroyed; it's very common."

He handed me the uniform, then went on, "Let's fix your hair a little. All the soldiers on the Russian front have been shaven bald because of the fleas and lice—let's just cut off your fringe."

Using a pair of scissors, he chopped off the crown. Then he gave me the numbers for his son's *Wehrmacht* unit and helped me memorize them. Once he was satisfied that I wouldn't forget, he covered me with the comforter, extinguished the lamp, and left, urging me to get as much sleep as I could.

I lay quietly in the darkness, peering through a crack in the shutters at a tiny star blinking in the cold night sky. Away from the city lights and industrial smog, the sky should have been brilliant with light, but tonight a dark cloud blotted out the heavens, leaving only the smallest gap through which this little spot of furious white burned like the sun.

I thought to myself how lucky I was: in a house, in a bed, food in my stomach. I felt protected; I had a friend. I coughed a little, and was reminded that I was still a long way from home and not in very good health. Tomorrow will be better, I told myself, and went to sleep.

Coming Home

For the next two days I rested, moving only to use the bathroom or to eat. The farmer was content to let me be, spending the mornings and afternoons in the fields and returning at night to prepare the meals. Over dinner, he occasionally coaxed a little conversation out of me, though I was still reluctant to talk because it brought me a lot of pain. I told him my name and the story of my imprisonment, and in turn he told me about the son he had lost in the war. We were lonely people, and we appreciated each other.

On the third morning, he woke me with a light touch on the shoulder. It was just after dawn, and I could hear morning birds outside the cottage. We ate a small breakfast—rolls and fresh milk, only a half hour from the cows and still warm.

"Let's get you dressed and we'll be off," he said.

With a little help from the farmer I slipped on the oversize gray-green uniform. The wool pants were unkind to my bruises, and my friend had to put a cloth with some ointment on it over my lower back to keep it from chafing. The uniform had been made mid-war and wasn't one of the proud, tailored models of the glory years—not that anyone would notice; the seams were all hidden in billowy folds that hung loosely from my tiny frame.

In addition to pants and shirt I wore a heavy overcoat and a billed cap with a high peaked crown in front and warm earflaps on either side. The shoes fit rather well, though they were a far cry from the metal-studded boots the German Army had provided a few years earlier.

As I sat next to the farmer in his wagon and watched the scenery glide past us, I noticed an eerie loneliness on the country road. We saw no other people, only the occasional wandering cow. The town was nearly deserted when we got there.

Years later, I read that Hitler had given up his aspirations of being an artist due in part to his inability to draw the human figure. His portfolio was filled with scenes of empty country-side and vacant cities. Fittingly, Hitler's vision of Germany had played out on all of its levels, including this one.

We found the milk truck easily, and I waited in the farmer's wagon as he loaded his five cans of milk. He explained to the driver that he had found a lost soldier near his farm, gesturing toward me. The driver nodded his understanding, apparently unsurprised by my appearance. He agreed to take me with him, and the farmer hoisted me up into the passenger seat of the truck, taking a firm grip on my upper arm as he did so and whispering "good luck." It was my face that he was staring into, but his fingers felt his son's uniform.

"Thank you sir," I mumbled as he closed the door.

I watched out the window as the truck pulled away and the man who had brought me back to life disappeared with the empty town behind me.

It was about an hour's ride to the city, with more of the same emptiness coloring the view out the windows. The driver didn't say much but seemed nice enough. He offered me a cigarette, which must have been a precious gift at this point during the war, but I politely refused, sensing the dull ache in my lungs.

The city was unreal. The transition from peaceful countryside to fire-gutted metropolis was gradual, but still dramatic. We dodged huge craters in the street, winding between bits of unrecognizable debris that marked our path.

Hungry faces looked longingly at the truck as it rolled by, including those of a few lone soldiers who were nearly as gaunt as I. The uniformed skeletons seemed to be wandering about without any particular bearing, looking for long-dead commanders to tell them what to do or where to go. In addition, there were a few patrolling soldiers of the *Volkssturm,* the People's attack force composed of men too old to enter the armed forces and Hitler Youth members who were still only children. These men and boys were the city's last line of defense against the approaching Russians.

I'd been right about my prison uniform—I saw several civilians wearing similar clothing, sometimes even tattered as badly as mine had been. Some people had improvised additional outfits, making shirts out of tablecloths and drapes, whatever they could find that would keep them warm.

The driver was nice enough to drop me off at the train station, and I managed with some difficulty to walk to the station house, where a sign informed me that I was in Gransee, some sixty kilometers north of Berlin and less distance from Ravensbrueck. I realized that guards would undoubtedly be looking for me, particularly along the major roads and in the train stations. I was scared; I didn't want to think about what they'd do to me if they found me. Finding a bench along a wall in a corner, I sat quietly and watched the other people bustling about in front of me, expecting to see the armband swastika of the SS drifting toward me at any moment.

While I was scanning the crowd, three young women approached, talking among themselves. I judged them to be about my age, and I stared at them the way a pubescent lad might have, though my curiosity was peaked more by simple awe than by any sexual interest—it had, after all, been more than a year since I'd seen a woman up close. One of them, a slender blonde, glanced up and noticed me sitting nearby. She returned to her conversation, which abruptly came to a halt, and the three were suddenly staring at me, shamelessly revealing in their faces a mixture of pity, guilt, and repulsion.

The blonde slowly stood up, then shuffled over to me, stopping at a distance safe enough that she didn't have to look directly at me while she spoke. "Can we help you, soldier?" she asked.

"I . . . uh . . . yes," I stammered, "I need a train to Duesseldorf—I belong to the Rhineland garrison."

She disappeared for a moment, checked at the ticket station, then returned. "Your train will leave at five o'clock for Frankfurt, where you'll have to change again. It'll take you seven hours to get to Frankfurt, and you'll arrive in Duesseldorf at about seven in the morning."

"Thank you," I said, hunting down a pair of eyes that were trying to avoid my own.

She turned to go, hesitated, then changed her mind and sat down next to me. Here was the very picture of Nazi ideology, Aryan womanhood honoring the protector of the Reich.

She made polite conversation, and I lied brilliantly as I answered her questions about my experiences in Russia and the valiant deaths of my comrades. Once she had satisfied herself that she had done her duty, she returned to her friends, and the trio left not long after, disappearing down the platform.

For the next hour I tried to relax, eating a bit of bread the farmer had given me and napping on my bench. I got up to use the bathroom. My vision went dark and I nearly collapsed, but I made it to the commode and back. I experienced an unusual feeling when I returned to the bench. I was afraid of sleeping. For some reason, the idea came to me that I would slip away and die if I let myself close my eyes again. It wasn't so much the idea of dying that bothered me—I was certain that I wouldn't live much longer anyway—it was just that I hadn't really finished the race yet; I hadn't gotten home. My escape wouldn't mean much if I'd risked my life for a few days of freedom on a farm and an afternoon at the train station. I wanted more. I wanted to get back to where I'd started.

The thought was repeating itself over and over in my mind, solidifying itself in the absence of other thoughts until it was suddenly cut short by a bolt of more immediate fear. A uniformed man was walking toward me. He was looking at me.

He stopped inches away. "Soldier, are you waiting for the five o'clock train?" he asked.

It took me a moment to get over my fear, but slowly I pulled myself together. This man was a railroad employee. He was just being helpful.

"Yes," I responded.

"Well then, you have quite a few hours left. Come with me, I have a better place for you to rest."

I followed him to a little room for employees only, littered with various pieces of railroad equipment.

"Don't worry about a thing," he said. "I'll fetch you in time to catch your train."

I thanked him profusely, secretly thanking him for not hauling me outside and shooting me, which had seemed a very real possibility only a moment earlier.

I sprawled out on the bench in the little room, a much wider one than I had been sitting on earlier, and covered myself with my trench coat. I was immediately asleep, forgetting my earlier fears, and though I must have slept for hours it seemed that only minutes had passed when I was revived a few minutes before five. My train chugged in at sunset, only a few minutes late despite the complications of the war. I found a seat and waited a few minutes before we departed.

In the gathering darkness I noticed that all the lights were extinguished in the streets and in the windows of the passing houses—air-raid precautions.

Two men behind me were talking, and I overheard snatches of their conversation, one saying, ". . . escaped from Ravensbrueck," and the other responding, ". . . SS . . . near Fuerstenberg."

I pretended not to have heard anything, feeling both relieved that the search was apparently concentrated in Fuerstenberg, a little town near the camp, and terrified that word had already spread to the civilian population that I was loose.

It took only forty-five minutes to reach Berlin. What little I saw was devastated. Nothing but ruins. I changed trains, boarding a rapid train that was already waiting when we arrived. After a quick blast of the whistle, the doors shut, and I was on my way to Frankfurt; so far, so good. The clacking of the rails soon put me back to sleep, and the hours passed uneventfully as we roared through the darkened countryside.

At 5:30 in the morning we entered Frankfurt station. The quiet dawn was disrupted by the shriek of the train coming to a stop, which in turn was swallowed, just as abruptly, by the meandering scream of an air-raid siren. A conductor ran through our car, shouting, "Leave the train immediately! Go to the bunker behind the station!"

I wasn't ready for a move. Something inside me was beginning a countdown, subtly letting me know that I was dying. I didn't think the train would get bombed, and I wouldn't have cared much if it did; I'd rather have stayed on and be bombed with it than go scurrying around in the cold and cramming into a bomb shelter with all the other passengers.

A woman passed me, saw that I wasn't moving, and started asking the men around her to help me off the train. Most of them were ignoring her in their rush to get out, but I didn't want to attract any more attention, and the thought of someone hoisting me up by my bruised and blackened arms wasn't very appealing, either. I got up and made my way toward the doors with the others, allowing the conductor to help me down the steps and onto the dimly lit platform. I couldn't see the exit, so I stumbled around blindly for a few moments, enveloped by the shrieking siren until the flow of people guided me outside and toward a concrete bunker.

Hobbling down the stairs and into the main room of the bunker, I found myself trapped in a sea of people, completely obscuring the floor. An old woman with two crying babies made a spot for me against a pillar, and I sat there quietly for the next hour, monitoring the sounds and vibrations of explosions somewhere in the city. Occasionally, a louder, close blast would shake the bunker, sending little particles of the ceiling crumbling down on our heads. The children whimpered and let out infrequent little screams, but throughout it all no one said a word.

I somehow felt like I was waiting for a funeral, huddling in a quiet church with mourners too embarrassed to speak, suddenly interrupted in their quietness by a drunken organist offering an entirely inappropriate marital march.

The bombing stopped. We sat perfectly still for a moment, half hypnotized by the silence. Slowly, people began to stir. The spell was broken. A loudspeaker blared from the station outside, "The train to Cologne will continue in fifteen minutes. All passengers please board."

As I rose from my cramped spot on the floor, immense pain coursed through my legs.

"Ah! Ah!" I blurted, slumping back to the ground.

"What's wrong?" asked the old woman who had given me the spot.

"My legs . . . they hurt . . . Ah!"

More pain appeared as I tried to straighten my knees.

"Here, let me see," she said, setting her two children on the floor. Very carefully, she rolled up my right pant leg. Two boys, each about twelve years old, stopped to watch on their way out of the bunker. The four of us grimaced at the sight of my leg, which was puffy and swollen. Examining the left leg, the woman found the bullet wound I had received in prison, which had opened again.

"I was wounded in Russia," I explained.

She started to ask a question, but decided against it. Instead, she said, "You need a doctor. Badly."

The idea of stopping now and looking for a doctor was out of the question for me. I was scared.

"No," I said, "I must get on the train; I will see a doctor later."

The two boys offered to help, eager faces betraying their lust for heroism.

"Yes, of course," stammered the woman, opting not to argue with a soldier.

Each boy grabbed a shoulder, helped me to stand, then dropped my arms over their backs. I was nearly a foot and a half taller than either of them, but they could have easily lifted my bony frame above their heads. They hauled me effortlessly back to the station platform, but we got there just as the train was pulling away.

They sat me on a bench and one dashed to the ticket office. He returned in a moment, took a few seconds to catch his breath, and said, "Another train leaves for Cologne in an hour."

They waited with me—waited *on* me actually, bringing me water and sharing the last of my bread with me. I could see in their eyes the sparkle of curiosity, but they restrained themselves from questioning me out of respect for my exhaustion and discomfort.

I've sat here before, I remembered, *Frankfurt to Berlin and then Sachsenhausen, then Fuerstenberg and Ravensbrueck, with those others—the Jew and the homosexual man and the other one, the one who commented on the Holy Trinity just before his chest exploded.*

I coughed into an already bloodied handkerchief, watching the boys' reaction as I did so. They were unafraid—perhaps even a little awed by the sight. Blood and soldiers go well together in young boys' minds. They had a certain adulation for me that was cute but scary at the same time—I wonder how they would have responded to my Ravensbrueck uniform.

My pant leg continued to rub against the open wound on my leg. It had never really healed properly, and I thought maybe it was a good sign that it was beginning to hurt again and swell up—it might mean that it was finally beginning to heal.

At 9:15 the train arrived, and the two boys who had

become my nurses helped me on board. It was crowded, so I had to stand.

The boys each had first-class tickets, but they were a little reluctant to leave me by myself.

"You're sure you can make it alone?" one asked.

"I'm sure. Thank you for everything—you've been very kind."

The darkened train departed with a lurch. I stumbled back as we pulled out of the station, feeling the pain again as I staggered to stay upright. After about twenty minutes, I began to feel incredibly weak, which is when I asked for a seat.

Then there was the argument as to whether I would be allowed to sit. A flicker of light danced before my eyes as a man worked his lighter, and soon I was sitting, mostly oblivious to the people around me. I watched the other passengers through a sort of haze; I meandered in and out of consciousness as we moved toward Cologne. One more train change and I would be home in Duesseldorf, but I wasn't sure I could make it.

Other passengers had to carry me off at the transfer point, hauling me along as my feet dragged on the ground. I prayed, "Please, let me get home before I die."

We reached Duesseldorf shortly after noon, and again I was carried off the train and across the platform. I tried to lift my legs a little to keep them from dragging on the floor, but they wouldn't respond at all, which surprised me as much as it scared me. I was taken to the Red Cross station, where the nurses laid me on a cot, took my temperature, and made a cursory inspection of my wounds, poking and prodding a bit to see if I still had sensation in my legs. (I let out a little yelp to let them know that I did.)

"We'll send you to the hospital as soon as we can get transportation," one of them said.

"No, no!" I objected, trying unsuccessfully to raise myself to a sitting position, "I want to see my folks. I've just returned from Russia and I haven't seen them in two years."

The two nurses exchanged glances, each expecting the other to make a decision. I took advantage of their hesitation.

"Do you know whether Chlodwigstrasse is all right? Has it been bombed?"

The older nurse, who seemed to be of superior rank, looked at me blankly. "Chlodwigstrasse? I don't know—everything's been bombed . . . oh, all right, I guess we can *try.*"

The nurses placed me on a stretcher and tightened the sheets around me almost to the point that I couldn't move—I must have looked something like a cotton sarcophagus as I was carried, straight as an arrow, outside and into the back of the ambulance, a converted Mercedes-Benz taxicab.

It was mid-February 1945, around five o'clock in the evening. Snow was falling. The ambulance driver knew the way, but had to make several detours to avoid streets too ruined to navigate. When we finally rolled up to the apartment building that had been my home, I could see only the lower floors from my vantage in the back of the car; the top two were blocked from view by the cab's roof. From what I could ascertain, the building looked to have escaped any direct hits.

The driver started to get out, intending to go and fetch my parents.

"Wait," I said. "Go up to the second floor, it's apartment 2. Ask for my father. If he's not there . . . well, don't tell my mother right away that you are bringing me home—I don't want her to have a shock."

He nodded understanding and then disappeared into the

building. Finding the door marked "Meyer," he lightly knocked. A few moments later, my mother's blonde head peeked through a little shuttered window in the door.

"Yes?" she asked.

"Is Herr Meyer in?"

"No." She was short, trying to keep the encounter with the stranger brief, lest it become unpleasant.

"You are Frau Meyer?"

Somewhat hesitantly, her curiosity peaked but her caution still intact, she replied, "Yes, what do you want?"

"I've brought you something."

Oh, of course! The packages Paul had been expecting from France had finally arrived! He would be quite pleased.

"Wait a moment, please," she said, leaving the driver in the hall for a few seconds while she found a cigar, the typical fee at the time for the services of a delivery man.

The driver gratefully accepted the gift, then somewhat reluctantly informed her that she should accompany him to his car. Her fears forgotten, my mother followed him outside.

From the ambulance, I could hear the door close to the apartment building and I turned to watch as they descended the icy steps and crossed the sidewalk.

Mother stopped a few feet from the ambulance, not seeming to notice it. She looked expectantly up and down the street, trying to spot the delivery truck.

The driver at first seemed unsure of himself, but after a moment caught the woman by the arm and directed her attention toward the Mercedes.

"What? I don't understand—" she said, bending over and peeking inside.

I stared back with warm, wet eyes, full of tears that I thought I would never cry. She didn't recognize me.

"Mutti—" I began.

Mother was turning back, stopped, turned around, and shot up against the window, pressing her face to the glass, staring hard.

"Mutti—"

"Walter?"

I was home.

Last Rites

No one moved.

Mother stood rooted to her spot outside the car, still peering through the window.

She blinked.

I looked at the driver, who had quietly accumulated some tears in his eyes, then back at Mutti. All at once, she regained her mobility, and with a flourish she took control of the situation.

She grabbed the driver by the arm and spun him around. "Quickly," she ordered, "go next door and get the neighbor to help us carry him up."

As he trotted off to fetch some help, my mother opened the car door and leaned in to examine her son. Somehow she saw through the purple, bloody skin, beyond the scars and wounds, and accepted the goodness that I was home and I was alive. She was confused, and there were questions that would have to be answered later, but for now she was content to take care of me and let me be.

The driver returned with the woman who lived next door, and my mother directed them to carry me out of the car and up to the apartment. Trying to help, the neighbor grabbed onto my legs, cradling them in both arms.

"Yieee!" I screamed. "My legs! Don't touch them!"

All three nearly let go of me when I yelped, but Mutti and the driver checked themselves and recovered before they could drop me.

"I'm so sorry, Walter, I didn't know," the woman said. The rest of the way up, she didn't so much as lay a finger on me, keeping her arms tucked up to her chest as if to restrain them from making any unexpected moves.

It took fifteen minutes to carry me up the stairs and into our home, everyone moving slowly and trying to handle me as gingerly as possible. Mother directed everyone toward the master bedroom, but I objected.

"No, the toilet," I insisted.

Unaccustomed to such delicacies, my stomach had decided to reject some fruit I had been given earlier. The trio got me into the room and seated me on the toilet, which was quite a feat considering the limited space for maneuvers, and my mother helped me get my pants down as the other two backed away, the driver leaving and the neighbor waiting in the hallway. As soon as they had left, the doorbell rang—three times in succession, my father's usual greeting.

The sound of footsteps trudging slowly up the staircase was audible from the bathroom, and mother opened the door and called out, "Paul? Is that you Paul? Hurry up, Walter's here!"

The footsteps stopped for a moment, then resumed in rapid thuds as my father bounded up two and three steps at a time.

"Where?" he blared, rushing into the apartment, hat in hand, still dusted with a light coat of snow.

He spotted me through the open bathroom door, a

crippled skeleton perched on a ceramic throne. He took two quick steps toward me, then faltered, stopped, leaned against the door frame.

"My god," he groaned. It had taken him a minute to realize the condition that I was in, and once understanding caught up with him, he lost control.

He cried, then Mutti cried, then the neighbor, who was still waiting nearby, started crying as well. I was too weak to cry, so I simply sat and watched and used the bathroom as the two women tried to comfort my father, who fell to his knees and stayed there for nearly fifteen minutes. When he got up, he walked directly into the bathroom, bent down, and embraced me, still seated on the toilet.

The police arrived shortly after noon the following day.

I heard my father open the door for them; I listened while he said flatly, "He's here, come inside."

Two men, each in gray uniforms, followed him into the bedroom. Kneeling next to me, my father pulled back the blanket, exposing my nearly naked body. It was an exhibition—an exclamation mark.

"Do you want to take him like this?" he asked.

The two officers were towering over me; they had approached the bed as they came in, as if to carry me off, but now they seemed to be shrinking away, not wanting to touch me. I recognized one of them, a fellow a few years older than I who had lived in the neighborhood when I was growing up. No doubt he, and probably his partner as well, remembered me by my reputation as an athlete—an association that clashed horribly with the image before them now.

"Come on, let's get out of here," the familiar one said.

The other looked at me a moment longer, then turned to my father and said, "We're sorry, very sorry."

They told him as they left that they would report that they didn't find me—a kind gesture but not particularly reassuring, as the standard procedure was to replace a missing prisoner with his next of kin.

My father, who had treated me so badly as a child and who I thought had hated me, conversed with the officers in the hallway.

"I'll go if I have to," he said, "but the boy stays."

Fortunately, Germany's downward spiral during those last months of the Reich had all but destroyed the typical fervor for law enforcement. People now talked openly about the "end of the war," a subject for which one could have faced death by SS firing squad only weeks earlier.

Duesseldorf's *Gauleiter* (political governor) had left town. Other officials had suddenly taken up humanitarian causes, trying to help the poorer majority of the people through the hard times, attempting to gain credibility in order to escape accusation when the Allies took over.

We were nervous for a few days, afraid that other officers would come and arrest either me or my father. The days passed, however, uneventfully. There were no callers, authorities or otherwise, and we sat together in the bedroom and listened wordlessly to the steady Allied bombardment that was blasting the city.

In addition to the air raids, the city was being shelled by artillery fire from only a few miles away. American troops across the Rhine occupied the old Roman city of Neuss. From there they had only a short push to overtake Duesseldorf, but had chosen to finish off its defenses first with a long-distance attack.

As I sat in my bed and clenched my teeth against the pain that caressed my legs with each jarring rattle of the building, it surprised me to think that there was still anything left for them to shoot at. Burning rubble covered more than half the city, and already two-thirds of the six hundred thousand inhabitants were gone (many had died, most had fled). As close as it was to the western border, Duesseldorf had been a favorite target of British air attacks long before D-Day. All told, before the first Allied soldier had set foot within the city, 75 percent of it had been destroyed.

The last flourish of bombing reached its peak shortly after my return, and my family was forced to move into a common bomb shelter under the building that had been converted from storage rooms in my absence. My condition worsened in the cold, cramped basement, and my father sought out a doctor. Everyone had gone underground or had left the city, so it was no easy task to find someone who could help me—my father had to give away a few packs of cigarettes in exchange for information that led him to a physician.

I didn't notice the doctor until he stuck a thermometer in my mouth—I hadn't seen him come in, and he may have already examined me a little before I was aware of him. He listened to my insides with his stethoscope, monitoring more precisely the rasping draw of breath that was audible even without the aid of the tool. He handled my legs, which had lost most of their feeling and were swollen to about twice their normal size, despite my malnourishment. (I was told several years later that the lack of vitamins in the camp diet had caused a deterioration of the nerve tissue, and that the run during my escape and the journey that followed had caused them to become inflamed and to balloon to huge proportions.)

After careful inspection of my limbs and wounds, the doctor rolled me over to have a look at the backside. I felt as he touched my lower vertebra, the coccyx—the bone was exposed, rubbed raw as the skin had worn thinner and thinner with the lack of food. It didn't hurt much when he touched my bones; I was too numb to notice.

When the doctor had finished, he pulled my father aside, and the two men talked in whispers for several minutes. They both left, and after a few hours my father returned, bringing with him a priest.

I wasn't surprised—I wasn't even scared really. I had felt that I was going to die for quite a while, and that it was finally happening was no cause for alarm in my mind. I was so tired.

Death will be like sleeping, I thought, *on a mattress so soft and comfortable that even my dreams will be free of the horror.*

While the priest prepared my body to receive the sacrament of the last rites, I heard my mother whimpering in the distance. Lifting one frail arm, I motioned her to come over to the bed. She bit her lip as she looked down on me, but I could still see the paths of tears that had gently rolled down her cheeks. Her face seemed so large, hanging over me as I lay there, the Latin droning of the priest floating in the air around me.

"Looks like I am going to leave you," I told her. "Let's pray a little."

She knelt on the floor, and I realized that the other people in the bomb shelter were doing the same. She clasped my hand, and together we prayed silently. The priest stepped around her as he continued with the ritual, and eventually he finished.

There was a candle glowing on a little table near the bed, and I watched carefully as the tiny flame danced and bowed, I felt the cool ashes on my forehead and the salt on my lips, and I watched the priest exchange a few words with my father as he left. Mutti was crying, someone coughed, and I died.

Death has become increasingly hard to define. In the few movies I had seen growing up, people died quite readily—a bullet wound or a knife in the chest would send someone into a brief death throe and, given a second or two at the most (though at that time a good, dramatic death scene was still acceptable in cinema) he or she would keel over and be done with it. As a child playing with my friends, I'd learned that in certain situations it was quite acceptable to "die" for ten minutes or so and then rejoin whatever war game we'd invented for the day.

And what is the end? When the heart stops beating? There are so many now who have been brought back from that point, revived with an electrical shock or stimulation of that red muscle we so often associate with the flow of life. When the brain stops thinking? Men lie in hospital beds for years without moving, never registering so much as a little blip on the scale that reads brain activity—we call them "brain dead," finding it hard to call them just "dead"—not when we can see the rise and fall of their chests and the surge of blood pulsing through their veins.

What made Lazarus more of a miracle than the resurrection of so many CPR recipients? Was it the time elapsed? How long until you're really dead? Five minutes? Ten? A day?

For me, it was an instant. A bleary, blissful second of milky peace on a midafternoon in March. There were no voices, no divine revelations—only a hazy freedom, a feeling of dizzy weightlessness that was reassuring in its unfamiliarity, and thousands of soft, golden lights—I was relieved to think that I was going someplace that was not part of what I had known,

not part of the daily pain and saddening cruelty to which I
had thus far been subjected.

I don't claim to know what happened to me after that; I
only know that I was, if only for a moment, beyond what I
had known, and that somehow I returned.

When I opened my eyes the following morning, I was still
in the bomb shelter, alive but still extremely unhealthy. My
mother stared at me for about six hours, sitting in a chair
at the foot of the bed and not moving at all, only blinking
and changing the tilt of her head about every twenty minutes
or so.

Wetting my lips, I tasted the salt that had been left there
by the priest. I tried to touch my forehead, to feel for the
ashes, to see whether anyone had wiped them off. My
mother caught hold of my arm and stopped me. She didn't
want me disturbing the sacrament—I was going to die the
way a good Catholic should die, despite my poor performance in the church. Still, there was hope in her eyes. She had
lost one boy already, and I could see in her gentle eyes
how badly she wanted to avoid losing another.

On the third day after the priest's visit, my father called the
doctor back.

"Frau Meyer," he explained, "his condition is no better. It's
only a question of a day or two—only a miracle could save
him. I'm sorry."

The priest returned, again administering the last rites. I
didn't understand why he had to do that again—once would
have been sufficient, in my mind.

Waiting for death was much less dramatic the second time
through, now that everyone was better composed due to
the rehearsal. Just as before, I was convinced that the end
was near, and I was resigned to accept it. About an hour after
the priest left, however, I felt a change developing in my

chest. Suddenly, I vomited violently, spewing nearly black blood onto the cellar wall, a good three feet from the bed. This happened several times in succession, until I thought I had none left to give. There was a revolution going on inside my body—a last push to retake the fort.

For the third time, the doctor was called in.

"This is a good sign," he said. "I think we can save him."

The fatigued faces of those gathered around the bed brightened a bit with the news, and quickly set about to make me feel comfortable and to bring me anything I needed.

"I'm thirsty," I croaked. "Water."

After losing so much fluid through vomiting, my body was demanding water. There was an intense burning that seemed to emanate from the center of my chest, and my nurses soon discovered that it would take more than a glass or two at a time to quench the flames. A flower vase about two feet high was filled with water and left next to my bed, and I emptied the vessel every half hour for nearly three days.

Then I developed an appetite. My mother had some juices left, squeezed from berries the previous summer, and the neighbors donated some eggs. Everyone deprived themselves so that I could eat, which I did with a gusto.

Finding that they had exhausted their food supplies without satisfying my hunger, the family set about attaining more. My father caught a stray cat, killed it, had my mother cook it, and fed it to me, not telling me what it was until later. After I had eaten that, he asked around about livestock and was told that there was a man not far off who owned a goat, but that he refused to give it up for any price. My father stole the animal, making the theft in the middle of the night despite the constant and seemingly random bombing that was covering the area. (He was later brought to trial for the theft, but the judge dismissed the case after hearing the circumstances, saying that he could hardly punish a man for trying to save his son's life.)

About a week later, while I was sitting upright in my bed in the shelter, hungrily eating goat meat and sucking down an inappropriately large volume of water, the shelling suddenly ceased. A few minutes later, there were brief bursts of small-arms fire, and then that was over as well. It was early April, and the Americans had entered the city.

New Flags, New Borders

We stayed hidden for a few days, not knowing how the Americans were treating the civilians they encountered. Were they like the Russians? Were they raping every woman they came across?

My father, however, decided that my need for medical attention outweighed any unsupported fears we may have had about the city's captors. Once we were sure that they had taken total control, he went out on the streets to seek out the commanding officer. After explaining my situation to the commandant, my father convinced the man to send a military ambulance to take me to an occupied hospital only five blocks from our apartment building.

I became something of a pet to the GIs in the hospital. They fed me from all sides, making a sort of game out of it. I didn't even move for the first few weeks—all I did was eat. Starting at seventy-eight pounds, I gained about two pounds a day while I was in the hospital. One of the men there commented that you could sit and watch me for a few hours and actually see me getting fatter.

The cuteness of watching "the little piggy," as they called

me, diminished a great deal when the other patients started noticing my vomiting reflex. It had been there the whole time—even at home with the little meals my parents had been giving me—the larger portions just made the habit more apparent.

The medical staff, however, were sympathetic to my situation, and they tried to help me unlearn the reflex, but were met with only partial success. They were not terribly concerned with that particular problem, though, and it was with a separate complaint that the American doctor addressed me at the end of my third week there.

"Walter, you've *got* to get up today," he said.

The doctor was good-looking, about thirty-five years old, and good-humored as well. There was a hint of sarcasm in his voice—I could tell that he thought it would be pretty comical to watch my pear-shaped body waddle around the room.

I grunted at him in response.

"Your heart is not going to keep pace with your stomach without some exercise. Let's see you stand up."

I lay still for a few seconds, and when I realized that he wasn't going to give up and leave me alone, I rolled over and decided to give it a try. Slowly, I lifted my legs over the side of the bed, stopping as I felt my feet come in contact with the cold floor. I looked around, noticing several nurses and orderlies who had stopped their business to watch the show.

"Come on," the doctor urged me, "stand up."

Holding onto the bedpost for support, I shifted weight onto my legs, and miraculously, I was standing. I smiled at the doctor, proud of my feat.

"That wasn't so bad, was it?" he asked.

"No," I answered, still beaming.

"Now," he said, "jump up and down thirteen times on your right foot."

He had to be kidding.

He wasn't.

"Come on, you can do it," he said, and I tried. It was more of a bounce than a hop, and I thought that I was going to fall over every time I shifted my weight, but I managed to get through about nine tries before the doctor burst out laughing, and I took that as a cue that it was all right to give up.

Once he regained his composure, the doctor patted me on the shoulder, telling me that I'd made a good attempt, and that we'd continue the routine every day.

It wasn't long until I could use a wheelchair, and I progressed to walking in stages. At first I was reluctant to leave the peace of my bed, contented that I was no longer starving, but the hospital staff pointed out to me that my arms and legs were as frail as ever, that only my belly had gained mass, and I decided that a little exercise might be warranted. Besides, I was getting bored staying in bed all day, and the prospect of exploring some new areas of the hospital was appealing to me.

It looked as if I was in for a special treat one day when a pair of orderlies offered to take me to a local pool for a swim. They thought the exercise would do me good, and they also guessed that I'd be eager to get back in the water after going so long without a swimming tournament. So I went along, put on my borrowed bathing suit, and let the two men lower me into the water—about six inches.

It was a temperate pool, kept warm by some kind of furnace that heated pipes running under the tiles, but to my still rotten skin it was as cold and invasive as newly melted ice. I screamed like a child, and the prospect of further pool adventures came to an end.

So I rolled, and later strolled, through the halls and rooms of the various wards in the hospital, stopping occasionally to sketch portraits of the staff and patients. Everyone there made an excellent subject—strong features, expressions ranging from the twisted snarl of agonizing pain to the gentle smile of a man who has had a bit more morphine than necessary. Everything about these men was different than what I was used to. What little I knew of the United States had come from the occasional movie I'd been able to afford as a youngster, which had included a few "Cowboys and Indians" shows. (One of my favorite actors in the genre had been Andy Divine, whom I actually met years later in Texas.) Naturally, then, I had a particular interest in a Native American GI from Oklahoma, whom I fully expected to let out a war cry and start a fire at any moment. I was sadly disappointed when I discovered that his primary interest while at the hospital was reading *Life* magazine.

I soon discovered that the Hollywood portrait of the typical American was lacking in other details, as well. I wandered outside one day, following a peculiar burning smell, to find GIs dousing leftover food with gasoline and setting it ablaze. Remembering the shortage of food among the local population, I started to protest, but the American GIs took a look at my robust folds, laughed at me and said, "Take a hike kid, you're the last one who should worry about starving."

Later, I overheard a couple of soldiers talking about their company commander, referring to him as a "fucking Jew."

I was shocked.

Weren't Germans the only ones who hated the Jews?

Major Herman, meanwhile, seemed to have prejudices of his own. He was not a doctor, but occasionally had reason to interact with the patients in the hospital, in which instances he usually gave me a wide berth, and when he did talk to me, he was short and sometimes even openly contemptuous. I was, after all, a German, a non-Jewish German, associated somehow, despite my individual circumstances, with the group that had slaughtered six million of his religious brethren.

I'd heard from Mutti that a few of the Americans had been beating up former members of the now defunct *Volkssturm*, calling them "Dirty Jew-killing bastards." I recognized the hypocrisy, but I kept my mouth shut—American hospitals were, after all, much more humane than the camps I'd been living in, and my overall impression of the Westerners was favorable. I missed them when they left, suddenly transferred to the Pacific. I'd made friends among them, and they'd piqued my curiosity about their nation, which seemed so different than anywhere I'd been before.

With the Americans gone, Duesseldorf quickly fell under British jurisdiction. England, always zealous for territorial conquest, was quick to claim its zone in the German land that was being divided like a pie among the four major Allied powers. I was content to let Germany go where she would; I only knew that the Second Great War was over, that I had lived through it, and that living through it wasn't enough—I wanted to live *beyond* it, I wanted to make life good again.

By the time the Americans had left, I was strong enough to return home. I'd weaned myself out of the wheelchair, but I still carried a cane to help me get around. Father and Mother had been to see me frequently while I'd been living with the GIs, but they were both elated with my return, the one showering me with hugs and the other commenting over and over again on the dramatic improvement I'd been able to make during my convalescent visit to the hospital.

Indeed, though I'd managed to even out the distribution of my newly acquired bulk, I was still fairly plump. And plump was a rarity.

Not long after my return, I went with my father to a neighborhood store for some supplies. There was a considerable line of people waiting to pay for their food and other necessities, and it was moving slowly since the cashier had to deal with people who wanted to make all sorts of barters as payment for their items. Father was getting anxious to get me back home to rest.

"Move ahead Walter, you can't wait in line all day—it's bad for your legs to stand so long," he said.

I was tired and my legs hurt, but I didn't want to make the other customers get angry with me by trying to jostle my way to the front of the line. Father had made a decision, though, and he rarely changed his mind.

We had just started to make our way forward when a man behind us made a comment about my bulk.

"Looks like *he* was eating well during the war," he said.

I almost fell over as my father grabbed my cane out of my hands. I watched him use it to beat the shopper hard.

"My. Son. Was. In. the. K! Z!" he screamed, punctuating each word with the thwack of the cane against the shopper's back.

The man stayed on the floor, and we had no argument with the rest of the line as we moved to the register, paid, and left.

We paid with government-issue coupons. However, we frequently used cigarettes or coffee instead. Cigarettes were hard currency at the time, easy to trade if you moved quickly—you had to get rid of them before they went stale. Coffee was even better; you could trade coffee for anything—butter, cigarettes, work, sex . . . whatever you wanted.

Nobody drank coffee in my family anymore.

Some American business geniuses (it was said that they were Jews, as most business geniuses were rumored to be) had installed an elaborate trading post in Frankfurt. Customers would come in, bringing with them cameras, jewelry, silver, china, artwork—anything of value—and exchange it for credit points. Then they'd climb the stairs to the second floor where they'd use their points to get cigarettes, coffee, butter, chocolate—things with current value on the streets. It was a good deal for the locals, in an immediate sense at least, since it was hard to procure a meal with a Leica camera, but easy enough with five cartons of cigarettes, which was the trade the Americans were offering. For the Yankees, it was a *great* deal. Within the American zone of occupation, they had a monopoly, and sometimes prisoners would even cross over from the English zone or the French zone to make a trade (though any goods they acquired were often confiscated at the checkpoints when they tried to get back to their families).

People were desperate for food. To get a ration card, one needed to present proof of work. At first, there were no jobs available, but then reconstruction began, and Germans were required to scrub bricks or clear debris from the streets.

Even with a ration card, though, meals were sparse. We were allowed fifty grams of meat products and twenty grams of fat/butter/oil per person, per week—enough for about one dinner. People began to experiment with alternative food supplies, first exhausting the resource that any neighborhood pets provided (cats and dogs disappeared first, then less conventional animals such as birds and fish), then substituting new ingredients for traditional recipes. *Reibekuchen,* potato pancakes that are particularly popular in Duesseldorf, were fried in cod liver oil when other oils became unavailable. It was easy to tell when someone was frying something in cod liver oil, because the strong stench of fish permeated the air several blocks away.

People responded differently to the food shortage. There

were those who hoarded food, stole, cheated. There were also those who sacrificed and shared. That was human nature.

In my family, we tried to help each other. I was bored with the dead city, so I made my contribution to family needs by bringing things home from out of town. I took every opportunity I could to travel, usually making excursions to Frankfurt in the American zone.

I'd received my ID papers from the Union of Former Political Concentration Camp Prisoners, which included a record of my TB history. The organization had gained a lot of political clout with the Allies since the end of the war, and those of us who had been through some sort of physical trauma in the camps were given special treatment. I was able to present my ID and ask for seats on buses and trains.

When I came home, I'd walk into the house lugging a laundry bag filled with cigarettes, coffee, and chocolate—a Santa Claus bearing economically sound vices. It was glorifying to make Mutti so happy, but I was frustrated in the knowledge that the family's real wealth was still just out of reach.

Like so many others, my parents had sent their valuables—china, linen, fancy clothes—to friends in the country, where their belongings would be safely distanced from the bombing. When the war was over, all of our prized possessions disappeared into the zone of Russian occupation.

Of course, there were ways to get them back.

Some of the little towns on the border had established a lucrative business in transporting groups from one zone to the next. Perhaps most famous in that respect was Helmstedt, a cozy border town not far from Braunschweig that had become known as the best place to pass through. It wasn't difficult to find a guide there to help you get where you wanted to go, and the connections that had been established with the Russian guards in the area were solid.

My parents were aware of my interest in crossing over into the Russian zone, but they didn't think I'd manage to pull it off.

"Don't be silly, Walter," my father had said. "They'll turn you around and send you right back home."

That was all the convincing I needed.

I got in contact with a guide in Helmstedt who put me on an eastbound train just inside the Russian border. I made a few connections, following the instructions I'd been given, and I was sitting quietly on a train bound for Suhl when I found myself surrounded by Russian soldiers who had boarded the Pullman.

I tried to look inconspicuous, and I glanced around with seeming disinterest, making it clear that I wasn't at all alarmed by their presence. It looked like they were going to leave me alone.

Someone grabbed my shoulder.

Turning around, I found myself face-to-chest with a huge soldier, who was babbling at me in Russian.

I don't know how they got the idea that I was a physician, but they communicated to me with hand gestures that they wanted me to inspect one of their comrades. The patient in question was afflicted by a large infected growth on the back of his neck that seemed to be giving him a lot of pain. I looked at the blemish for a moment, then back at the other soldiers. They clearly did not want to be disappointed.

Mostly using sign language, I asked for a sharp knife. I was given a military blade, and I went to work. I went through my pockets and produced a match. I struck it, then held the blade over the little flame to disinfect it.

First I tried to puncture the growth, but I realized that a larger cut would be necessary to allow all of the fluid to drain, so I made about a quarter-inch slit across the top of it. There was a lot of pus, and almost instantly the patient was thanking me. I poured vodka over the wound, and I joined the soldiers in a brief celebration.

I managed to locate my mother's friends and get back most of what we'd sent away, and I was on my way back to the British zone in about two days. I managed to cover the first dozen miles of the return trip by day, but was forced to finish the journey on foot when the trains were unexpectedly stopped and rerouted, a regular occurrence at the time.

I joined a little caravan of about fifty others like me, and we managed to cross the border unimpeded, though we saw a few Russians with machine pistols who had been coerced in one way or another into not noticing us.

I arrived home carrying a suitcase in each hand.

I can remember watching as mother lovingly fingered the treasures I'd brought back for her, holding each item up to the light for inspection before clutching it to her bosom. Father stared at me and shook his head in surprised approval. For the first time in my life, he showed that he was proud of me.

Once word got out that I had crossed successfully, I was regarded as an expert. And, though I didn't really have much experience, I had learned a few important things about the Russians.

The Soviet Army had pooled its manpower from the hinterlands of the country, pulling in thousands of boys from Siberia and the wasted farmlands of the northeast. These men were from a different world, and it was not uncommon to find that one of them, in his confusion, had washed in the toilet and done his business in the bathtub.

German women were of special interest to all of the

invading forces, but whereas the Americans tried to lure them into sex with goodies, the Russians had a reputation for simply raping them. Many of the soldiers were adolescents, and their appetite for things sexual had endeared them to pornography. I kept a good supply of nude photos in my pockets to use as bartering chips. In Erfurt, I was stopped by some Russian soldiers who thought that I was a member of the *Wehrmacht,* wandering around and looking for my family the way so many others did. Their hostility seemed to disappear as I produced my arsenal of sexually explicit photos. It wasn't long before they were sitting with me and laughing as they admired their new treasures, patting me on the back as a compatriot in a nasty little secret.

While the British were busy helping us to rebuild our city, the Russians were busy destroying the countryside. For some reason, many of them had decided to lead horses into the oat and wheat fields to let them graze. The farmers sat complacently and watched as their beautiful fields were trampled and eaten.

Talking with a friend of the family in Suhl, I asked him how he got such a nice gold pocket watch.

"A Russian soldier gave it to me," he said, "in exchange for my chrome one."

"Why would he do that?"

"Mine was still ticking, and this one had wound down. They like to listen to the 'tick-tock,' and they don't realize that you have to wind it to keep it going."

Another friend told me a story about a man who'd been riding a bike without holding on to the handlebars. A Russian stopped him, thinking that it was a special bike, and tried to ride it himself without holding on. The soldier fell over and the owner of the bike took a beating for having "tricked" him.

For whatever reason, I seemed to have had better luck in my encounters with the Soviets, and it wasn't long before rumor escalated my brief adventure in the east into a full-fledged cloak-and-dagger story.

It wasn't long before I was approached by my friend Inge, a young lady who lived in my neighborhood. She wanted me to escort her to a town near Zwickau in the Russian zone. I was a little wary of making another trip, because by that time the Russians had developed a fairly efficient routine of kidnapping Germans.

In Russia, there was a need for educated manpower in practically any field. With Germany and her collegiate-minded populace at her disposal, the Russians were able to meet their needs by the trainload. Hundreds of men were herded onto freight trains and shipped to Russia, where they were sorted by profession and set to work for their captors. And those who didn't turn out to be engineers or doctors were still useful, since they could always be sent to a quarry.

A similar process had been adopted by the Americans—U.S. officials would search out the best German minds, physicists and economists and the like, and "invite" them to come live in the States. The typical invitation usually included a university appointment or a government-funded research project—good incentives to geniuses otherwise trapped in a newly flattened country.

However, it was difficult for me to turn down such a lovely girl as Inge, so we joined another group of Germans crossing at Helmstedt.

We crossed on foot, intending to walk to a ditch along the railroad tracks a few miles away and meet a guide who would get us onto a train headed for Zwickau. We managed to walk the first hundred yards or so, saying nothing and listening to the crunching of dead leaves under our feet.

"*Stoy!*" someone shouted.

We turned around and found ourselves confronted by five Russian soldiers with machine pistols.

We stared at them for a moment, blinking stupidly, and they stared back at us. Then they formed a sort of semicircle around our group and led us to a house they had taken over—the location and the decorations inside, antlers and a bearskin rug, seemed to suggest that the place had been owned by a forest ranger.

Nobody really tried to communicate, and we huddled together in the center of the living room—not sure whether we were supposed to sit down. The Russians watched us for a moment, trying, I suppose, to decide if there were any men in our group who might present a problem. When they were satisfied that they had total control, a handful of them each selected a German woman to take outside and rape.

They weren't hostile about it, they just meandered through our ranks until they found a lady that suited them, grabbed her by the arm, and led her outside. The men in the group stood still, quietly eyeing the carbines.

The women were scared, but the first one or two were so shocked and confused that they didn't put up any sort of protest about being separated from the rest. They didn't scream at first.

Screaming always makes bad things happen faster.

One woman, though, had thawed. She moved haltingly as a large, roundish soldier tugged on her arm. She stared back at her husband with a question in her eyes.

"It will be all right," he said.

She seemed satisfied with that, and she started slowly off with the guard. Then—I don't know why—she stopped and turned around. Urine was running out the bottom of her pant leg.

She screamed.

Then everyone started screaming.

The soldier grabbed her, holding her chest to his own, and strutted out the door with her, pressing his pelvis into her and lifting her feet a few inches off the floor. Her husband lunged forward, but two of the German men closest to him held him back.

The door slammed shut behind the Russian soldier and the screaming woman, cutting off her cries with the sharp report of oak striking oak. The screams in the room devolved into whimpers until all that was left was the angry, bewildered breathing of the husband.

The remaining guards came unstuck from their posts and started to examine those of us who were left. Inge had not been taken; she was still with me. A soldier who spoke some German asked us who we were.

"I'm a doctor," I told him. "This is my wife, Inge—a nurse."

Together with some twelve other potential candidates for Russia we were led away, supposedly to the regional headquarters in Marienborn.

There was only one guard now, an elderly man walking behind us and prodding us along with his gun. I judged by the way he walked that he was a little drunk.

We walked reticently for about ten minutes, the silence only broken by the noise I made in occasional fits of coughing. Inge put a hand on my shoulder and asked me if I was all right.

"Yes," I said, "I don't feel well but I think I'll be okay."

We continued for perhaps another five minutes, and when I felt the time was right, I threw myself to the ground, shaking and convulsing, writhing spasmodically on the ground.

"He's having a seizure!" someone shouted.

The soldier ran over to me, leaned over my wiggling body and tried to see what was wrong.

As soon as it was in reach, I grabbed for his gun. He still had a firm hold on it, and there was a terrible moment when I thought I'd made a mistake. With a sharp jerk, though, I was able to pry it free, and I fired three rounds into his belly.

We all started running.

Inge and I stayed together. Desperately, we made a giant, frantic loop around to avoid the area surrounding the ranger's house and the nest of Russians. We didn't stop until we'd made it back to the British zone.

Nobody crossed at Helmstedt for a while after that.

About a month later, a wealthy lady who was a friend of the family came to me and asked me to recover some of her belongings in the Russian zone. Things had quieted down a bit, and I'd heard that it was possible to pass near Bad Harzburg without too much difficulty, so I agreed to help her out.

She'd sent her valuables to a farmer relative's house in a little village not far from Leipzig, and I was able to find the place without incident. I was invited to celebrate *Erntedankfest,* Harvest Thanksgiving. The farmer and his wife treated me to some of the finest goose meat, along with potatoes and vegetables. They seemed to like me, and we had a nice conversation after dinner about nothing in particular.

The next morning I took a look at the boxes I'd been sent to fetch. There were four of them in all, but I didn't think I could carry more than two. I'd have to come back for the others later.

I wasn't in any particular hurry to get back to the British zone, so I thought I might try to visit some old friends in the city. The farmer lent me a bicycle, and I set off for Leipzig.

For some reason (there was usually no reason at all), I was

stopped by some Russian officers. Since I couldn't communicate with them, I just followed complacently as they led me to a little building they'd taken over. There were a few rooms in the basement that looked to have been wine cellars at one point. They locked me up in one of them.

I sat there for a while and started to get nervous. I didn't know how they could have found out, but I had a nagging suspicion that they somehow knew that I was the one who had shot the soldier a few weeks earlier.

They left me alone until about one o'clock in the morning, which seemed to them to be a good time to interview me. A look at my identification made them realize that I was from the British zone. They asked me a few questions in Russian, and I guessed that they wanted to know what I was doing in Leipzig. There were basically two assumptions they could make—I was either trying to smuggle things out or I was a former German soldier who was trying to find some relatives.

"Konzentrationslager," I explained, trying to dispel any notions they might have had that I was a Nazi. They seemed to understand what I was saying, but they didn't have any reaction to it—I was still just a prisoner who had been captured in the wrong zone.

I tried to impress on them that I loved Russkies and that I was a simple artist and not at all dangerous, but they didn't care much. After a while they went away.

It didn't look like I'd made much progress.

A few different officers came in about an hour later, and we had a session that was basically a repeat of the earlier one. After that I was interrogated by a young Russian woman who spoke German fluently. She seemed a little dubious of my promise that I was just an artist—I think that she would have preferred to have caught a spy or a former Nazi commander. I had her bring me a pencil and some paper and I drew her portrait, which seemed to satisfy her. I asked if I would be allowed to leave soon, and she replied with nothing more than an enigmatic smile.

The following day, around noon, a guard came into my makeshift cell and sat down next to me on my cot. He was a big brute, probably around 280 pounds. He smiled tooth-lessly at me. He had a pencil and some paper.

For the next week, I was visited about three times a day by various Russian soldiers, and I made around thirty sketches. They were fairly nice to me; there was plenty to eat and drink and everyone was cordial and appreciative of my talent. I think they finally let me go because they felt sorry for me being locked in the basement. The bike I'd been riding when I was captured had disappeared, but the Russians confiscated a better one for me before I left.

The farmer and his wife were surprised to see me when I got back—they had figured that I'd run into some trouble and gone back home. Over lunch I explained everything to them, apologized for losing the first bike, and made plans for my return trip.

I was ready to leave that afternoon, but I had a bit of an accident in the outhouse. I'd gone into the foul-smelling little building and was pulling my pants down when my wallet fell out of my back pocket and disappeared down the hole. I stared after it, thought about going in to find it, threw up, and left without it.

I managed to get back across the border without my ID.

Leaving Home

By the time I had returned home, my father had started a job as an interpreter with the British occupation force. He had been cleaning bricks for a few months, knocking the old chunks of mortar off so they could be used again as the British soldiers directed the reconstruction of the city.

Educated men like my father didn't have a function beyond what they could do with their hands and their backs during reconstruction. You're an engineer? Good, clean some bricks. A poet? Here are some bricks. The war had reduced us to a system of almost perfect equality among the classes. A few men landed jobs in the motor pool, which was no great achievement, either, but at least it didn't involve as much manual labor.

Father had found a use for his talents even while doing such mind-numbingly simple work. Many of the English officers spoke at least some German, and many of the German citizens spoke English fairly well, but there were always little moments of difficulty when one group or the other tried to communicate. Father simply stepped in and bridged the gap, and when the British soldiers realized what a valuable re-source they had in him, they took him on as a full-time aide.

Even with the nicer job, it was hard to supply the family with decent food and clothing. The black market was less prevalent under the British than it had been under the Americans, so it was necessary to rely more heavily on the painfully inadequate ration system.

I managed to make connections with some confined but enterprising Jews in a resettlement camp near Frankfurt. They were willing to procure the occasional block of butter or pound of flour in exchange for a generous supply of cigarettes. I got along well with the Jews, who seemed to share a certain kinship with me based on our similar wartime experiences. It was good to have friends who were able to help you out.

One of my friends after the war was a French physician who worked for the United Nations Refugee Agency (UNRA). One day he asked me whether I knew how to drive a car.

I had no idea.

"Sure," I said.

He wanted me to pick up his Renault at a garage in Frankfurt and drive it back to Duesseldorf for him. He gave me the details, and I headed off the next day. I found the garage, found the car, and took a few minutes to figure out which controls did what.

I promptly backed into a wall.

There was no damage, but I had quite a bit of trouble maneuvering out of the building. The garage owner asked me several times as I was fidgeting with the clutch, whether I in fact knew how to drive.

"Of course," I assured him.

It was approximately 150 miles to Duesseldorf, long enough for me to get acquainted with the Renault. The vehicle had military plates, which I was able to use to get free fuel at military gas stations. At one station not far from Frankfurt, a couple of M.P.s decided to question me. Unfortunately, I didn't have any documentation with me for the car—nothing even showing that I was allowed to drive it, let alone get free gas—so I bolted.

I was down the road a good hundred yards before they even got in their jeep, which was no match in terms of speed for the little roadster. I quickly outpaced them, but I kept up speed even once they were out of sight so as to avoid any possibility of being caught.

It was then almost impossible for me to stop when a bicyclist tried to cross the street in front of me. I swerved to avoid him, but caught the edge of his bike pedal. He went flying maybe ten feet into the air and landed in a ditch on the side of the road. I pulled over and leaned out the window to have a look at him. He was pretty banged up but very much alive. The M.P.s were just appearing in my rearview mirror as I started off again, and this time I managed to lose them for good, so I assume they must have stopped to help the bicyclist.

I got the car back to my French friend a few days later.

"Any problems?" he asked.

"Not really," I said.

"Did you hear anything about an accident with a bicyclist?"

"Hmm? No."

Back home in Duesseldorf, watching the city slowly rebuild itself, I looked around at the schoolteachers who had become prostitutes and the lines of former Nazis queuing up to denounce other former Nazis, and I realized that Germany had become pitiful, and that reconstructing the buildings and cleaning the debris out of the streets wasn't going to erase the shame, wasn't going to bring the pride back. When my father got a job for the French as chief interpreter in Mayen, I was glad to leave with him; I had had enough of Duesseldorf.

Father had been offered the job primarily in response to his continuous help to French civilians while he was stationed in Lille during the German occupation. His benefactors decided to give me a job as well, as a courier. The job had a lot of benefits.

I was provided with a 500 cc BMW motorcycle, and cruising around on the bike in my khaki shirt and pants and a black beret, I looked more French than German. I didn't say that I was French, but I didn't deny it, either. The ID I was given even had blue, white, and red stripes in the background. I had instant access to military trains—the M.P.s would come through the compartment asking for passports, and I'd flash the ID card and smile at them. "Thank you," was all they ever said.

My courier route ran from Mayen to Bad Ems, another French post. One time while I was wandering around in Bad Ems trying to find some goodies to bring home for the family, I happened upon a couple of French soldiers who were beating a German man. The poor guy had given up trying to defend himself, and he just stayed on his belly and let them kick him in the ribs over and over, whimpering a little but obviously resigned to the fact that the soldiers would keep at it until they got tired or bored. I walked over and tried to look disinterested as I asked the French soldiers what the man had done.

"He stole some of our bread," one of them told me.

"I see," I said. They continued to rough him up. "Have you

seen the newest pictures?" I asked, producing a little stack of pornographic photos from my pocket.

The two soldiers landed another half-hearted kick or two, then huddled over me to have a look at my pictures. They were giggling and pointing and haggling over prices with me while the German fellow staggered to his feet behind them and wandered off. Through the narrow gap that separated one Frenchman's shoulders from the next, I watched him go. It's too bad he didn't get to keep his bread.

I don't know exactly when or how I got the idea, but I think it must have been because of the sadness in Germany that I decided to leave. I couldn't stand living in such un-promising desolation—I wanted to go somewhere where I could still have a chance at some new adventures. Though I hardly knew anything about the Americas, they somehow seemed a logical destination.

I visited a former teacher of mine—I remembered him telling me once that he had relatives in America. I explained my situation to him, and made it clear that I intended to get to America somehow.

"North America or South America?" he asked.

It really didn't make much difference to me, since I knew equally little about either part of the world. So I wouldn't look bad, I answered, "North America."

"Then I'm afraid I can't help you," he said. "My relatives own an estate in Argentina, in South America."

"I can't believe that you are leaving," my mother said.

I had told her that I was going to a water polo meet and that I would be back within a week. I explained that I would need my good suit for a victory dinner after the game. She was getting suspicious.

"There are usually no sporting events at this time of year, Walter," she said. "Are you sure you're telling me the truth?"

I looked away as she tried to find my eyes, paused a moment, then flashed back a smile.

"You need a little vacation from me. Don't worry, I'll be back soon."

She embraced me and pecked out the sign of the cross with her little hand, tracing Jesus onto my forehead, my chest, and my shoulders. "God bless you," she said, then let me go. She stood at the open window and dried her tears with a handkerchief as she watched me walk away, waving good-bye every time I turned my head until I was out of sight.

Seven years would pass before I would see her again.

Father was not at home when I left. I had visited with him the day before, and I'd revealed my plans of reaching America. He gave me the names and addresses of some friends in Belgium and France, and with unemotional detachment he explained to me that he would not try to stop me because he was sure that I wouldn't be able to leave the country without the right papers. Still, he offered a few words of advice.

"Everyone you meet you should consider with much caution and expect the worst. If he turns out good, you'll have a pleasant surprise; if not—that's what you expected!"

There were no tears. Father was certain that I'd be back in a few days.

All things considered, the prospects for a successful journey looked pretty bad. The German people made an easy transition from wartime regulations imposed by their own government to postwar regulations set up by the occupying forces. Each zone had its own rules, but some were universal throughout occupied Germany, like an ordinance forbidding Germans to be on the streets past 10 P.M.

It was late afternoon when I reached a friend's house outside of town. I traded my suit for two cartons of cigarettes
and waited until 6:30 to cross the Rhine, when there was still
enough light to see where I was going but not enough to
make me too visible. I hitchhiked to Aachen, an old Roman
city on the German-Belgian border where Charles the Great
was buried. It had been about two-thirds destroyed during
the war. The truck driver who had picked me up had to
make quite a few detours to avoid roads that had been
bombed and were off-limits. By the time I reached the city it
was about 10:30, so I had to be careful not to attract too
much attention.

I managed to get to the train station, and I struck up a conversation with a railroad employee. I spoke in broken German, sometimes stumbling over the vocabulary, feigning a
heavy French accent. I explained to the man that I'd been
held in Germany as a prisoner of war and that I had met a
German woman whom I wanted to marry.

A pack of cigarettes helped create a friendly atmosphere.

"I'm not supposed to be here—I had to cross into Germany without papers," I explained. "I need to get back to
France quietly."

More cigarettes.

"Wait a moment," he said, and disappeared.

About fifteen minutes later he returned, and walking close
to me but not looking at me, he whispered, "There is a freight
train on platform 5C."

"When does it leave?" I asked.

He stepped away for a moment, looking in another direction as if he were interested in something else, and then whispered to me, still avoiding eye contact, "Soon. Hurry up but be
careful. The freight cars are empty and the doors are open."

I slipped him another pack of cigarettes. "Thanks," I said. "One more thing. Don't get into the last car."

It was close to midnight.

I saw a uniformed man climb into the caboose of the train at 5C. I waited a moment, looked around, then slowly opened the door of one of the empty cars and disappeared inside. There was a whistle, and the train began to move.

In a few minutes I was out of Germany, a geographical Houdini.

The locomotive came to a halt a couple of hours later in Herbesthal. I waited for the railroad employee to leave the caboose before I opened the door to my car. It was raining heavily when I stepped out onto the Belgian mud that was forming along the sides of the tracks.

I knew the area. The people here had changed their national identities several times over the course of history. They spoke French and German, one better than the other depending on the age of the individual.

A friend back home had given me the name and address of a relative who owned a small farm in Henry-Chapelle, some three miles from Herbesthal. I found his place around dawn. A dog barked when I knocked on the door. A window opened, and the farmer stuck his head out and yelled at me.

"Who is it? What do you want?"

"Mr. Charbon?" I asked.

"Yes."

"My name is Walter Meyer. Your nephew in Duesseldorf told me that I could find you here. I'm trying to get to Brussels."

He seemed rather irritated.

"I'm sorry, but I can't let you in. The police are checking

constantly for Germans. Wait and let me make some sandwiches for you."

He disappeared, and I sat on the doorstep and waited for a few minutes while he got the food. After a while he opened the door and handed me a little bundle that contained a few sandwiches and some apples.

"If you wait over there," he said, pointing to a wooden stand along the side of the road, "you can get a ride to Liege on the milk truck. The milkman comes at about 5 A.M. to pick up the cans."

I nodded understanding and started to walk off toward the road. Mr. Charbon called after me, "Don't tell anyone that you are German!"

The rain had almost stopped. I was sitting on the side of the road and munching on the farmer's gifts when the milk truck rolled in. It was almost identical to the truck that had carried me away from Ravensbrueck a few years earlier.

The driver was a happy fellow. He whistled a lot, not really sticking to any particular melody. He was glad to have company along for the ride. I helped him load the milk cans into the back of the truck as we came to the various pickup points.

We didn't talk much. When I told him I was French he apologized for speaking the language so badly.

It took about an hour to get to Liege. The driver let me out at an intersection in the center of the town and wished me well. I could hear him whistling as he drove off.

I kept going, hitchhiking through Namur to Brussels. The people who gave me rides were all nice folk, and I had several different opportunities to try out different stories about who I was and where I was going.

"Vous êtes français, n'est-ce pas?" ("You are French, aren't you?") one man asked.

"Comment savez-vous?" ("How do you know?")

"On le voit tout de suite" ("One can see it right away"), he assured me.

It was a wonderful compliment to be mistaken for a Frenchman, and it strengthened my confidence.

The driver of the last car, the one who dropped me off in Brussels, gave me two Belgian francs and told me which streetcar to take to Schaerbeck, a suburb of Brussels where some of my father's friends lived.

It was noon, July 8, 1947, when I rang the doorbell at the house of Mr. and Mrs. Isbecque. My father had saved Mr. Isbecque from the Gestapo, warning him that he was under suspicion of spreading anti-Nazi sentiments and encouraging him to leave. The family was eager to show their gratitude by taking good care of me. I spent two days in Brussels, and I was flooded with invitations to visit the tourist attractions, sample the best foods, and spend time with the family. I was even awarded a bottle of Coca-Cola—an unheard-of luxury back home.

As hospitable as Belgium was, I was packing my bag by Wednesday night, ready to move on. Mr. Isbecque leaned on the door frame and watched me as I collected my few toiletries and the two or three changes of clothes I had brought.

"You should go back home to your parents," he said.

"Maybe I will," I answered. "Maybe I'll bring back some gifts for them from America."

He smiled at me. I think he would have come along with me for the adventure if the circumstances were a little different.

"Bonne chance, Walter," he said.

Mr. Isbecque was a distributor of small agricultural machinery. One of his clients had a tree nursery in Peougy on the

French-Belgian border. Isbecque's brother, Pierre, was to take me to Peougy and introduce me to the nurseryman.

Mr. and Mrs. Isbecque embraced me warmly as I left, filling my pockets with a little money and some sweets. I walked to the streetcar that would take me to the Chaussée de Mons, the highway that connected the two countries. It was July 10.

With two trucks I hitchhiked to Ponneai, where Pierre lived. His son was home on vacation from college. The three of us ate a leisurely dinner, finding little to talk about but enjoying a comfortable silence. Pierre explained how to get to the nurseryman's house. I assured him that I would find it easily and that there was no need for him to escort me all the way.

"Very well," Pierre said. "You'll be expected."

After dinner, in the late afternoon, Pierre's son walked me to the bus stop.

At 6:15 I left for Rougy, close to Cleharies. On the way I saw Belgian police escorting lines of German prisoners.

Rougy was the terminus. Someone showed me the way to the *pepinnieriste,* the nurseryman. He seemed pleased to see me and invited me to join him for dinner. So far, things were going well for me. There is very little to complain about when you have good company and free food.

"You are German?" he asked me.

"Yes," I said. We were speaking French.

"I once lived in Germany—for five years," he said. "It is a beautiful country."

"Yes it was," I replied.

After dinner we went outside. It was just after sunset, and the sky was still a soft pink, clouds floating in the air like the angelic puffs decorating the backgrounds of Renaissance paintings.

"Isn't it beautiful?" he asked me.

"Yes," I said, "very beautiful."

"They have skies like this in Germany sometimes," he said, "when the sun goes behind a mountain."

"The sky was like this a lot in Duesseldorf during the war," I said.

The tree farmer nodded at me and smiled.

"From the fires," I said. "They'd bomb the city on the other side of the Rhine, and the next day the sky would light up from the reflection of the fire eating up the buildings and houses on the other side. It was beautiful. Just like this, really."

We crossed into France after dark.

By 10 P.M. I'd walked the four miles to Saint-Armand, four days out of Germany.

The Secret Handshake

The town was dark. There were no trains or buses at that time of night.

I found a small hotel and knocked on the door. Nobody answered.

A couple of Algerian miners wandered by around midnight, and I followed them to a little hovel in a run-down part of town a few blocks from the train station. I watched them converse for a moment with a woman who seemed to be the proprietor of the establishment, then saw them disappear inside.

I walked purposefully toward the little building and tried to talk to the woman. She said something, but I couldn't understand the dialect. I smiled at her.

She motioned for me to follow her as she led me to a small room with a mattress on the floor. She smiled and disappeared.

I found a curtain in a heap on the floor, which I used as a blanket. I slipped my wallet under my pillow, though I didn't really think it was necessary—I felt somehow secure here. I lay awake for a long time, thinking about nothing and breathing the quiet air of a city dead with sleep.

The next morning I asked the woman how much I owed her, but again I ran into the language barrier. She seemed satisfied with a pack of cigarettes.

The nurseryman had traded me some French money for the Belgian money I'd had when I reached his house, with which I was able to buy a bus ticket to Lille. The ticket cost me eighty-five francs, and I was ready to leave at 7:30 A.M. I talked to the driver during the ride, and he suggested that I get off at Rue Nationale, where I crossed over to Rue de Pas. I found the home of Joseph DeDonker, who'd been my father's chauffeur during the German occupation.

"Yes?"

It was a woman who answered the door, who I guessed must have been DeDonker's wife.

"Is Mr. DeDonker here?" I asked.

"Yes, one moment."

She disappeared, and I could hear her muted voice calling inside: "Joseph, Joseph, there's someone here to see you . . ."

DeDonker was a little cautious at first, not recognizing me and not used to getting many visitors.

"My name is Walter Meyer," I told him. "I'm—"

"Come in! Come in!" he said. "How is your father?"

The DeDonkers offered me a cup of coffee and a chair in their living room. Mr. DeDonker had a lot of questions about my family and the war, and I answered them and gave them the details of my trip into France.

"You made it all this way without papers? That's quite a feat," he said.

I took a sip of coffee and reacted with a jerk. It tasted strange.

"It's chicory," Mrs. DeDonker explained, "everyone adds a little chicory to the coffee in France."

Mr. DeDonker had apparently heard quite a bit about me from my father, who had told him about my arrest and subsequent disappearance during the war. I gave him the full story of my life in Ravensbrueck, my escape, and my postwar adventures. He told me I should write a book about it.

I stayed with the DeDonkers for two weeks. While I was there in Lille, I had the opportunity to meet several of my father's old friends. Paramount among them was Mr. Pra, who had hidden in my father's office for weeks after escaping from a Gestapo prison, and who now enjoyed a certain amount of influence in the Prefecture, the government of postwar France.

Mr. Pra was an intelligent person, a speculator on world affairs and a man with considerable allegiances throughout Europe. Having heard the propositions of men such as Henry Morgenthau, who had recommended that Germany be converted into an agrarian nation, Pra had taken the initiative to prepare a French ID card for my father to use if the situation at home became insufferable.

While we sat and shared a bowl of soup together at his house, Mr. Pra handed me the ID card.

"Ghastly photograph, don't you think?" he asked.

The facial close-up of my father stared back at me in black and white, painfully serious.

"That can be fixed," I said.

That evening I removed my father's photo and replaced it with one of my own, filling in the missing corner of the official seal with an indelible pencil. When the touch-up was complete, I had become Claude Paul Meyer, from Colmar, Department Haut Rhin—an Alsatian. The Alsace-Lorraine story worked well for me, providing a good explanation for the hint of a German accent that colored my otherwise very convincing French.

Mr. Pra helped me the following day to organize a few packages to send home to my parents. Included were some soaps, coffee, noodles, and some other goodies, with a brief note explaining my current situation and assuring them that I was doing well. For me the little letter was something of a victory flag, letting my father know that I was well on my way to reaching the goals he had deemed impossible only a few days before.

Mr. Pra thought that we should try to find a legitimate permit that would allow me to stay in France. Together we went to the Prefecture, to whom Mr. Pra explained my situation. The civil servant smiled back with the distinctly phony grin that is shared commonly by government receptionists and tax collectors. "I see," he said when Mr. Pra had finished with the story.

"Do you think you can help us?" Pra asked.

"Let's play the piano first."

By this he meant fingerprinting. They took a full set of prints before we were allowed to talk to the "higher-up," the next man in the chain of command.

Mr. Pra explained the situation again. There were no smiles this time. When Pra had finished speaking, the French official took a long, weighty sigh. He sounded like a disappointed parent. When he finally spoke, he directed his words mostly at Mr. Pra.

"Because of his father's outstanding reputation among the French citizens, I am disinclined to put this boy in jail. Instead, we'll give him the opportunity to return to Germany." He paused for a moment, glanced at me with a flicker of repulsion in his eyes, then continued, "If he really wants to come back to live in France, I suggest that he present himself in Baden-Baden, and show them the letter we'll prepare for him explaining the situation—of course, it may take them some time to process such a request. If you come by in the morning, we'll have the letter and a train ticket waiting for him."

I'd been glowering at the man since he started talking, and it was quite obvious that I wasn't too pleased with his decision. He turned to me and stared right at me as he continued. "If this boy has not left the country by Tuesday, we will be forced to follow *alternative procedures*."

Mr. Pra thanked him and the two of us walked defeated out of the Prefecture. Mr. Pra seemed genuinely disappointed and a little surprised that things had not gone more smoothly for him. Still, he wasn't up for any additional bickering with the Prefecture. We returned the following morning to pick up the train ticket and the letter, which read:

> *Au cas ou l'interessé obtenant l'autorisation de pénétrer regulièrement en France, visa a soliciter à Germersheim, la situation serà immediatement regularisée par la Préféc-ture du Nord.*
>
> In case the interested party obtains a permit to enter France regularly, with a visa to be obtained in Germersheim, the situation will be put in order immediately by the Administration of the North.

In other words, the letter was completely useless.

Mr. Pra thought that we might have better luck with the Swiss consul, an acquaintance of his.

The consul was a very slow-moving, gentle old man inclined to scratch at the top of his oak desk with the edge of a fingernail every few minutes. He listened to the story, offered a bit of a tired smile, and then made a great production of standing up and waddling off for a few minutes before returning with some paperwork for a *permit de séjour*, which I filled out while he scratched purposefully at a different spot on his desk.

Within the hour we had made the request for a temporary residency permit and received a *Réfus de séjour*, a residency denial. The consul didn't seem surprised by this, but he offered an apology and his card and suggested that I speak with his colleague in Baden-Baden.

He sincerely regretted not being able to help.

I sincerely didn't want to return to Germany.

We returned to Mr. Pra's apartment.

I sat quietly on a sofa in the living room while Mr. Pra scribbled a few things on a card for me. When he'd finished, he handed it over to let me have a look.

It read:

> Mr. Jean Pra, *Directeur du Club Economique de France*, asks all of his brothers in the G.O.D.F. to help and assist his good friend, Claude Paul Meyer at all times.

Mr. Pra was a leader in one of the freemason lodges, and he had decided to offer me the protection of the Grand Orient of France.

"Give me your hand," he said.

He clasped my hand firmly in his own, and showed me how to identify myself by applying pressure repeatedly with one finger while shaking hands.

"Thank you," I said.

"God speed, Walter. Tell your father I did my best to help you."

The next day I left, taking with me Mr. Pra's masonic message and the newly altered French ID card. I headed for Malo-les-Bains on the Atlantic coast. There I met with my father's former secretary and some of his friends, with whom I stayed for a couple of days before heading on to Paris.

I remember that it was July 30 when I arrived in Paris. I managed to contact a few of my father's acquaintances, and they were all eager to help me out with food and money without being asked. They wanted to show me the city, but I wasn't too interested. I had decided to head for Spain as soon as possible. My plan was to cross into Spain, then continue to Portugal and on to South America. I didn't think that my inability to speak either Spanish or Portuguese would be much of a problem.

I took a train to Hendaye on the Spanish border. I had made friends with a young Frenchman on my journey to Paris, and he'd promised to meet me in Hendaye and help me cross over into Spain. Somehow we missed each other. I needed a new plan.

At a coffee shop I ate a little breakfast, some biscuits and jelly and a cup of coffee. I watched the woman working behind the counter as I ate. She was in her mid-forties, and her considerable cleavage had caught the attention of the three or four male patrons of the shop that morning (including mine).

"Excuse me," I asked her, "do you know of someone who could help me get across the border? I'm willing to pay."

"Yeah. I know someone who can help you out," she said, returning my stare. "Wait a minute and I'll give you his name and address."

She vanished into a back room of the little building and returned with a piece of paper with a name scrawled on it.

"Go to the train station. I'll give him a call and tell him you're coming."

"Thanks," I said.

I shot her a smile on my way out the door.

At the train station the police were waiting for me.

"Do you have papers?" I was asked.

I tried out my ID card for the first time.

The officers seemed to be pretty interested in the card, turning it over and taking a close look at it. They weren't quite sure what to make of it.

They took me to the *Sûreté,* the security office, where I sat with a crowd of Germans, Spaniards, and Italians who had been caught without papers and were waiting to be processed and sent to jail. At 11 A.M. I was allowed to see the *commissaire.* The sergeant-investigator wore civilian clothes and a large mustache. He led me to the second floor to question me. My wallet had been taken from me earlier, and he turned it over now in his hands.

My German ID was still in the wallet; I kept it in case I needed to prove who I really was in an emergency. It was sandwiched between lots of other scraps of paper, mostly French, that had accumulated over the past few weeks. He examined each item he came across with scrutiny, posing a few questions every time he encountered something interesting.

"And your father's name?" he asked.

"Paul Meyer."

"And your mother?"

"Henriette Meyer."

"And *your* name?"

"Claude Paul Meyer."

"And you were born where?"

"In Colmar, Department Haut Rhin."

He had just reached my German ID card when the phone

rang. He got up, answered it, and stared out the window as he talked and laughed for a moment with someone who was obviously a friend on the other end. I started to reach across the desk to retrieve my wallet. The *commissaire* turned ever so slightly . . . then pivoted back to face the window again. I retrieved my wallet, watching my hands shake uncontrollably as I fumbled quickly through it, found the ID card, removed it, and dropped it down my shirt. I returned the wallet to the desk just as the *commissaire* was saying good-bye.

He hung up the phone, returned to the table, and resumed the interrogation. He looked at the wallet for a moment before picking it up.

Did I put it back in the right place? Had I disturbed something on the desk?

The *commissaire* grunted and retrieved the wallet. After a few seconds he discovered the card Mr. Pra had prepared for me.

"Are you a mason?" he asked.

"Yes," I replied.

"Faites vos signes!" ("Make your signs!") he demanded.

I shook his hand the way Pra had taught me.

The *commissaire* didn't seem to be quite convinced, so I explained to him that I had attended several masonic meetings with my friend, Mr. Jean Pra, but that I was too young to become a full member, and that I definitely would soon become a regular member of the Grand Orient of France.

I left the *Sûreté* with the *commissaire's* hearty *"bonne chance."*

Sailor and Artist

Not long after the incident with the *commissaire,* I decided that it was time to get out of France. A border crossing from France into Spain presented some new problems for me. Since I had no contacts and couldn't speak Spanish, I figured that the safest route would be via the Bay of Biscay, swimming out on the French side and looping around to return on Spanish shores.

I followed the coastline for a day, approaching the border around sunset. It was easy enough to spot; a high chain-link fence ran straight up to the shore, then continued off into the water as far as I could see. The tops of the fence were decorated with bushy coils of barbed wire. Apparently, my plan had occurred to others before.

I didn't see any guards, but it would take me at least a couple of hours to circumnavigate the fence, and it was possible that a patrol might come along and check the area sometime later while I was in the water. I would be literally a sitting duck.

By the time I had had a look around, the sky was already growing purple as the sun dipped below a black sea bowing over the horizon. I waited, and when the sea and the sky faded to the same shade of black and melted together into one starless wall, I stripped off my clothes, rolled them into a ball, tied them on my head, and stepped into the water.

It was cold. There was no sand, only porous rock and sharp pebbles. I couldn't seem to keep the stones from creeping between my toes and staying there as I waded toward the fence. I had decided to follow the path of the fence until reaching its end, guessing correctly that it was rooted to a shelf of rock that allowed me to wade most of the way rather than swim.

The water was choppy. Small, triangular waves buoyed me up and down as I gripped the shelf of rock with my toes to hold on. Rocking nauseously with the momentum of the waves, I was knocked off balance by a large one that caught me in the chest. I wobbled for a moment and then fell into the fence. There was no chain link here, only barbed wire. I winced as the little metal thorns bit into my thigh and belly, but there were no clothes for the barbs to catch onto, so I was able to get free of the fence quickly and keep moving.

With the sting of the salt water worrying my new wounds, I moved more slowly along the fence. Every few minutes I would stop and scan the shores behind me, looking for border patrols from either side that might have seen me. But there was no one.

I found the fence's edge, a tangle of loosened wooden poles and barbed wire matted with clumps of seaweed. I had to swim a bit to get around it. Once on the other side, I was eager to get back onto land and forced myself to move more quickly.

I allowed myself a few minutes of rest on the Spanish beach, then dressed and got as far away from the border as I could. I found a road and waited for a ride.

I hitchhiked to San Sebastian. For two days, I wandered around, trying to figure out how to get to Portugal. Many of the Spanish people living in the border towns could speak French, but it was hard to remain inconspicuous with a foreign accent.

I'm not sure who turned me in, but one of the people I had talked with in my first days in Spain must have been a police informer, because I was picked up by the police one afternoon while I was negotiating the price of some oranges at a fruit stand.

I spent two days in a small prison before someone who spoke French turned up to interrogate me. The Spanish *oficial* was a likeable person, very plainspoken. He had gentle wrinkles around his eyes that were the product, I am sure, of smiling. He told me that I was going to be put on a train with some other prisoners and sent back to France within a few days.

"Look, friend," I told him, "once I get back to France they'll just toss me back into another prison. I haven't really done anything too terrible, you know, that's just how it goes. But really, you can't have too much interest in seeing me go from one prison to another, can you?"

"Unfortunate for you," he said, "but better in France than here in Spain where you can't even speak the language, eh? And besides, what can I do about it? You can't stay here."

"One prison is the same as another," I said, "I'm no criminal. Why don't you let me go? I'll go back to France on my own and I won't cause any trouble. There's no reason for me to stay here any more."

Much to my surprise, I was issued a certificate of *salvo conducto* (safe conduct) and turned loose on the streets.

True to my word, I headed back to Hendaye.

I spent the next day relaxing on the beach, trying to gather my thoughts and come up with a plan. About one o'clock in the afternoon I had a bit of a panic when I saw the *commissaire,* the same man who had interrogated me a few days earlier, strolling down the beach.

"Vous-êtes toujours ici?" ("You are still here?") he asked, surprised to see me still in the city. I explained that I was staying for a few days to take advantage of the good weather, and that I would be leaving soon. *"Bonne chance,"* he offered, waving.

I took the train to Bordeaux. The French doctor whose Renault I had endangered back in Germany had given me the name of his family in Artigues, about twenty minutes away.

On the train I spotted a pair of attractive young ladies and quickly decided to change seats to be nearer to them. One of them was talking about Germany. It seemed she had a job working for the French military there.

Somehow I managed to work my way into the conversation, and things went pretty well for us. I learned that the girls were on their way back from Biarritz, where they had spent their vacations on the Atlantic beach. The one who had been stationed in Germany was named Claudette. I explained to her that my father, who was Alsatian, was working as an interpreter under the same employ. The conversation became a little flirtatious, and I noticed that Claudette's friend was squirming around a little, trying to find a polite way to get me to leave the two of them alone.

It was two o'clock in the morning when we reached the station in Bordeaux. I volunteered to carry Claudette's suitcases. The other young lady had made arrangements for her brother to pick her up, but before she left she glared at us disapprovingly. I smiled back at her and waved.

When I had offered to carry Claudette's luggage, I hadn't known what I was getting myself into. I ended up carrying her suitcases more than three miles. We talked along the way. I found myself staring at her small feet as we trudged along. I timed my speaking with my breathing so I wouldn't reveal how out of breath I was—I wanted to make it clear that carrying the suitcases was easy for me.

To reward me for my assistance, Claudette's parents invited me to spend the night with them at their country place. The weather was bad the following day, and I was invited to stay another night. I explained to them over dinner that I was tired of Alsace and that I was eager to find a job on a ship. Claudette's father listened attentively and interjected a few words of advice from time to time as the mother brought in the food from the kitchen.

A large bowl of artichokes was set down in front of me. I took one and put it on my plate. I stared at it for a minute while Claudette made a few remarks about the sad state of the German economy. I'd never seen an artichoke before. Once I'd established that I was really meant to eat the thing, that it wasn't some kind of overgrown garnish, I stabbed it with a fork and tried to slice a chunk loose.

Everyone laughed at me. Claudette showed me how to eat one properly, and I became quite a fan of the unusual vegetable.

I stayed a while longer with the family, and Claudette promised to visit my parents upon her return to Germany. I learned later that she had been unable to get away, but she had sent a nice letter to my folks letting them know that she'd seen me and that I was doing fine in Bordeaux.

I found my doctor friend's father the following afternoon, an engineer with good connections in the port. At his farmhouse I ate escargot for the first time, this time waiting to see how he approached the little globs before making any embarrassing mistakes.

Mr. Sedeuil helped me to secure my first job on the docks. I was one of a group of men known as mules. Trucks would come in every day with cargo for the outgoing ships, and we'd stand below and catch as giant sacks were dropped onto our shoulders from the top of the vehicles, then load them onto a conveyor belt. The sacks sometimes weighed as much as 150 pounds.

I remember watching one day as the man in front of me caught a sack of grain dropped from about four feet above his head. His knees buckled under the weight as it landed on his left shoulder, and it slid out of his grip as he fell to the ground. Crying, he stood up and looked at the puddle of grain around his feet that was spilling out of the ripped package. He'd have to pay for that.

Though the work was intense, the pay was good, 663 francs a day, enough to pay rent. I found a room at a little hotel called Fleur Jasmin near the place Gambetta. My new home was in the attic, were it was sometimes very hot, but I didn't mind much—no level of discomfort could keep me from sleeping after a hard day's work unloading the trucks.

I took my lunch with the other mules at a little restaurant a few minutes away from the docks. We ate heartily, devouring every morsel that was placed before us. There was always a pitcher of red wine in the center of the table, and I watched as the other men passed it around, poured a little onto their almost empty plates, swirled it, and drank it. Nothing was lost that way, and it kept the dishwasher's job easy. The weekends were my days off, and I'd invariably spend them on board the ships, painting portraits of the sailors. I was fascinated by these men, who were always moving on, changing their scenery from week to week and remaining the same through it all—immutable but migratory. It was good to draw their faces.

One afternoon, around five o'clock, some sailors I'd been chit-chatting with invited me to join them for a glass of wine. One of them, a lisping fellow named Blaise, suggested a little café with a brick patio.

We'd been at our table for about ten minutes when a young lady came in with a merchant marine officer, arm in arm. She was beautiful. Her eyes were black pearls. Her hair was black satin. She and her companion seemed to know Blaise, and they approached our group to say hello.

I stared.

She tried to ignore me at first, but I was so forceful with my eyes that she was compelled to turn her head and glance at me every couple of seconds. She didn't want to look at me, but her eyes did, and she was fighting with them.

"Are you Russian?" I asked.

"What?" she responded, stiffening and backing away from me.

"You have an Asian face. It's very nice. I thought you might be Russian."

Everyone thought I was being perfectly absurd.

"If you want to know so much about me, you should read this," she said, handing me a newspaper she'd been carrying under her arm.

The headline read:

BARBARA GOES FROM PORT TO PORT TO SEE HER HUSBAND AGAIN AND TO PAINT.

Blaise teased me about it after Barbara and her friend had left. "Too bad for you, eh?"

But I wasn't defeated yet. I thought maybe we could find some common ground on the basis of our artistic interests, so I asked around and found out where she was staying. I called her room from the front desk. There was a bar in the hotel, so I asked her if she'd join me for a drink.

There was a pause on the other end of the line. She took a breath. I could hear her tongue rolling in her mouth. "Okay," she said. "I'll be down in a few minutes."

When she showed up at the bar she was wrapped in a brown shawl, her hair pulled back and covered with a kerchief.

"How are you?" I asked.

"Fine."

"I read the article. It sounds like you're a busy woman—traveling around all the time and still trying to keep up with your artwork. Don't you get tired of always being on the go?"

"No."

"You know, I'm an artist too. I draw portraits for the sailors. Maybe I could show you some of my drawings—and you could show me some of your paintings?"

"Maybe."

"You're not very talkative."

"No, I'm not."

Her fists were clenched at her sides, her white knuckles contrasting with the dark colors of her dress and shawl.

"You think I am a detective? A secret agent maybe?"

"Why would a detective be interested in me?" she asked.

"I am German," I volunteered.

That caught her attention. She stared at me, studying the lines in my face. She took a sip of wine.

Barbara Gvozdavo-Golenko was born in Finland, the daughter of a Russian general and a Russian mother. Her father had been head of the Secret Service before the revolution, and had fled to France with his family like so many White Russians when the Czar's empire started to crumble.

When she was old enough, she fell in love with a Frenchman and became French by marriage. During the war, her father was accepted into the German Secret Service, and Barbara became a nurse. When the situation deteriorated for the Nazis, her father joined up with the Americans for a while until they detected his double play.

I never knew for sure whether her story was true, but I can't see any reason for her to have made it up.

I visited her often. Eventually we worked together doing portraits for cigarettes or cash. Our styles complemented one another, but whereas I used pencils, she painted in thick oils, smearing great globs of violent color onto the canvas until she had produced something bold and fantastic.

Sometimes she would play the piano for me at her hotel. She was an excellent pianist. Chopin was a favorite for her, and I loved to listen to her pounding out arpeggios and letting her fingers trill over the keyboard in fast runs up and down the scales. The newspaper article she had shown me when we first met was misleading. Barbara was divorced from her French husband. She had a lover, a U.S. Merchant Marine officer whom she called "husband" when she had been interviewed. When the American was away, I took his place. It was a strange relationship, but a happy one.

One evening a few months after I had met Barbara, I was working by myself in a little bar, painting and doing sketches for the sailors, when a tipsy captain came in and asked me for a portrait. He ordered a couple of drinks and proceeded to suck them down while I did a sketch. By the time I had finished the drawing he was completely plastered.

"Now that," he said, "is bloody beautiful . . . Fantastic!"

I thanked him and collected my fee. It was getting a little late, so I started putting my things together and getting ready to go home.

"Where are you going?" the captain asked.

"Thought I'd go home."

"Why don't you stay a while? I want to buy you a drink for making such a beautiful drawing."

I accepted the offer. The captain seemed to be very interested in me. He wanted to know all about everybody in the bar. I told him I wanted to be a sailor.

"Well, hell," he said, "I'll hire you as a seaman soon as you're ready."

He also promised to give his boat to the bartender if he died at sea. He had another cocktail.

"Claude," he said, "you're a hell of a guy. I have to get back to the ship now, but I'll be sure to come find you next time we come through."

He stood up to leave and promptly fell to the floor.

I helped him back to his feet, but he couldn't seem to get very far on his own before stumbling over something or getting himself turned around, so I propped him up and dragged him down to the docks. I helped him get on board and led him to his quarters, where he abruptly collapsed on the couch and passed out. I was pretty exhausted after having practically carried him all the way from the restaurant, and I sat down on the foot of his bed for a few minutes to rest.

When I woke up the next morning the *Silver Ocean* had already let the coast slip over the horizon. We were out to sea.

"Hey. Hey, wake up. Who are you? What are you doing here?"

It was the captain. He was jabbing me in the ribs with an empty bottle of Scotch to wake me up. He wasn't too alarmed to find a stranger in his bed. I explained what had happened, and he smiled understandingly.

"Well then," he said, "you were kind enough to help me, so I'll see if I can do a little something to help you." He opened his desk, rummaged through it for a few minutes, and produced a little booklet.

"What's your name?"

"Claude Paul Meyer."

He scribbled in the booklet.

"Here, take that," he said, tossing it into my lap. "You want to be a sailor? You can start this afternoon."

His present was a seaman's book, which was carte blanche for finding a job on just about any ship in Europe. I was a sailor.

I spent the next few days washing dishes and getting used to life on board the ship, which wasn't particularly good—the captain and his rabble were the most disorganized group of drunken seamen I'd ever run into.

When we visited Casablanca I decided to stay behind.

New faces, new attires, different languages, a multicolored society—Casablanca was colorful and loud and dirty. One of the most interesting buildings in town was the women's penitentiary. Some talented businessman had converted the prison into a popular bordello. Sailors and other visitors had to leave their belongings at a security office and pay a fee before they were allowed to see the women. They'd walk through the cell corridors and pick an appealing woman. Curtains were drawn. I assume the women made a small percentage of the profits.

I remember walking past this place and being impressed by the long line of uniformed sailors gathered outside. There were two young boys running around and trying to peep through the entrance—there was nothing to see.

I wasn't making much money so I decided to look for work. Without much effort, I found a job on a Danish ship sailing for La Rochelle in France. The crew were a happy bunch, almost eery in their incessant smiling and good humor.

I ran into some trouble as we came into port—French police decided to check our crew list and discovered that there was a Frenchman aboard. At that time, it was almost impossible for a French citizen to leave the country without an assortment of special permits. I, of course, had none.

The crew did their best to help me out—someone even told the police that I'd jumped ship—but I was soon discovered and hauled away by two officers. One held me by the cuff of the shirt while the other clamped a hand around my wrist and shouted incoherent insults into my ear. I took a look at this second man, stared at his yellowing teeth and the scars that adorned his lower lip, and asked him what the penalty was for sailing out of France without the proper papers.

"Thirty days in prison," he told me, "and I wouldn't be expecting to work on a ship again if I were you."

Automobiles zipped past us on all sides as we walked through town, and we had to stop frequently and wait for a break in the traffic. At one intersection, just as we had stepped into the street, a motorcyclist sped around the corner and came right at us. The policemen let go of me and jumped back to the safety of the curb. I ran the other way as the motorcyclist skidded through the street in a shower of bright orange sparks.

There was a lot of confusion following that. The police ran over to see if the man was hurt, and a huge crowd gathered in the street, creating a wall between me and my captors. I backed away tentatively, expecting at any moment to be remembered and pursued. Once I had put a little distance between me and the crowd, I turned and ran. I ducked down an alley and hid behind some discarded wooden crates. I sat down, caught my breath, and waited. When I felt satisfied that the police hadn't followed me, I stood up, brushed myself off, and returned to the port.

I found a Dutch ship that was about to sail for Le Havre. I asked to speak to the first officer.

"I got sick," I explained. "My ship left without me."

"And she was on her way to Le Havre?" he asked.

"Yes sir."

He frowned. "Well," he said, "I suppose we have room for one more."

In Le Havre I was reunited with Barbara, who had followed her "husband" there to catch a glimpse of him before he set sail again for Tunisia. She and I worked together in the bars and the International Seamen's Club as portrait artists. Sometimes we would work the same bar on a busy night, but more often we would split up—one working ISC, and the other working one of the other large bars nearby—and then pool our earnings. That way, neither of us would go home with empty pockets unless both did.

On one occasion, while I was working alone in the ISC, I noticed a heavyset sailor staring at me while I sketched.

"You like the portrait?" I asked him.

He nodded.

"Would you like me to make one for you?"

"No. Not yet, go ahead and finish the others—I'll just watch for a while."

This wasn't too peculiar; I was used to having an audience when I sketched. People like to see the progression of the portrait from the rough, black shapes to the finished likeness. Half of my business came from sailors who were enough intrigued by the evolving shapes on the paper to be compelled to buy one for themselves.

I went on with the portrait.

After a few minutes, I realized that the sailor had started to move a little closer. Perhaps he was trying to get a better look at what was going on. Glancing up, I noticed that a few other patrons in the bar were watching me. They were smiling.

I took another look at the overweight sailor. He stared into my eyes and grinned sheepishly.

"Um," I said, "it makes it hard for me to concentrate on what I'm drawing when you sit so close. Would you mind?"

He frowned, offended. There were giggles from the bar.

I finished the portrait and decided to leave for the evening. On my way out the door, I was grabbed from behind. Two fatty lips pressed against my cheek, leaving behind them wetness and the stench of alcohol as they were removed. I struggled to break free, but was held fast by two mammoth, hairy arms. I yelled for help, but no one seemed to be interested—the only people who took notice were a few drunks who thought the whole situation was pretty funny.

One of the giant hands snaked its way up to my face, play-ing over my lips and cheek. Finally I found a finger and bit down hard, tasting the metallic tang of blood filling my mouth. The finger didn't come off, but there was a crack of bone suffocated almost instantly by the louder noise of a scream. The man released his grip and I darted away, the echoing laughter of the ISC faintly bounding after me.

A few weeks later, as Le Havre began to lose its charm, I talked to Barbara about returning to Bordeaux. She had tem-porarily lost track of her husband; sometimes his letters were separated by weeks as they meandered through international postal services. I convinced her to go with me, however, and we resumed our artistic activities in the same bar where we had started off.

We had an uneasy relationship with the barman. We were popular with the customers, and we managed to bring in fairly large crowds, but the bartender, a Dutchman with a big nose, was constantly suspicious of me. Customers would ask me about my peculiar accent, and I would explain that I was Alsatian, and I would notice the bartender staring at me from across the room, creasing his eyebrows and pursing his lips. His distrust made me nervous, but the job brought in a lot of money and allowed me to make some good contacts among the sailors.

On one occasion, an American captain talked to me for a while in the bar and told me that he'd be willing to take me on as a sailor, even take me to the U.S., provided I get a valid passport. I wasn't about to pass up the opportunity, so I had some photos made and visited the police station the following morning. I was asked to fill out an application addressed to the prefect, leave the photos, and return the next day. A taxi driver, after a nice tip, testified that he had known me for a number of years as a law-abiding citizen, and Barbara stated the same. I was French, the son and grandson of French, and I eventually received a *certificat de passeport,* with which I could apply for a regular passport at the passport agency.

At the passport agency, the man at the desk took a look at my certificate and noticed that I had previously lived in Lille.

"Excuse me for a moment," he said, disappearing into a little office.

"Where are you going?" I asked.

"I need to make a phone call."

I strained to hear the almost inaudible words of the passport agent speaking on the phone from the other side of the door suspended in the air around me, of which I could only make out ". . . I see."

After a few moments the door opened.

I shrugged my shoulders quizzically at the passport agent, as if to ask, "Everything check out okay?"

"The agent in Lille is busy at the moment. I'll have to call him back in about an hour. You're welcome to wait, if you'd like."

Reaching across the table I retrieved my certificate. "Thanks, but I have a few things to attend to. I'll come back later."

I was eager to get as far away from the passport agency as possible. The last thing I wanted was to be around when the local police had a nice chat with the officers in Lille and compared notes on me. (Years later, when I talked again with Mr. Pra, I discovered that the passport agency had given him a call to check on my story. He had confirmed everything I had said in my application. Had I stayed and waited at the agency that afternoon, I would have gone home with a bona fide French passport.)

Things were getting more lax in terms of international travel within Europe. By this time, Germans were starting to turn up periodically in the bars—the French government had started to issue work permits allowing a few Germans to come into the country legally. Of course, since I didn't have such a permit, my position in France was just as precarious as ever.

One day, as I was making a sketch in the bar in Bordeaux, a young German man walked in and sat down to have a drink. I recognized him! He had lived not too far from me in Duesseldorf.

I tried to keep my face hidden behind the canvas, peeping out at him every few seconds. I reassured myself with reminders that years had passed and that perhaps he wouldn't recognize me out of the context of the old neighborhood. I went on sketching.

After a few minutes, he stood up and started heading for

the door. Just as he was about to make his exit, he turned around and looked me straight in the eyes.

"Walter!" he said, *"Welche Freude, Mensch, wie geht's Dir?"* ("Such joy. Man, how are you?")

My jaw dropped. I shot a horrified glance at the bartender, who was already en route to the phone to call the police.

In a panic, I threw my sketch pad to the floor and ran from the building, nearly knocking over my stupefied German friend on the way out the door.

I ran straight to the railway station and onto a rapid train heading for Paris. I did not stop to buy a ticket. Barbara had left for Holland a few days earlier to meet up with her man again, so my only concern was getting as far away from the Bordeaux police as possible.

I sat down and caught my breath as the train pulled out of the station, and I stared out the window as we moved away, waiting to see if the police had followed me and if they would stop the train.

"Votre billet, s'il vous plaît" ("Your ticket, please"), I heard from somewhere behind me. The conductors had started to collect the tickets.

Standing up, I made my way to the bathroom. I locked myself in.

There was a knock on the door.

"Your ticket, please."

"I am sick," I insisted.

"I will wait."

A few minutes passed, and then there was another knock. I realized that there was no use in staying locked in the bathroom, so I opened the door.

"Listen," I said, "I am a sailor who got drunk. My ship left for Antwerp and I have to catch it. Please, help me to get there."

The conductor was unsympathetic.

"Do you have papers?" he asked.

"Yes," I said, handing him my ID and passport certificate.

He took them without looking at them and said coldly, "I'll see you in Paris."

The French have a simple and effective method of dealing with stowaways. When the conductors find one on board, they call the railway police at the city of destination (Paris, in this case), and announce the arrival of a "customer," who is greeted by the police when he gets off the train.

I was taken to the police station in the fifteenth arrondissement. The conductor handed my ID card and passport certificate over to the police, who gave them a cursory inspection at the station. My occupation was listed as artist-painter, which didn't jibe with my story about being a sailor who had missed his boat.

There were four cells, all reeking of urine because there was no running water. I sat in one of these for a while, cradling myself for warmth. Watching my breath float away from me in icy clouds, I tried not to think about the cold. I decided to try to sleep a bit, reasoning that I wouldn't be so miserable if I weren't fully conscious.

Sleeping proved exceedingly difficult, however, since I couldn't find a comfortable place to rest my head. I tried leaning against the walls and wedging myself into the corner of the room, but always the bite of the cold concrete against my back kept me from nodding off.

After about an hour a guard came by to ask me a few questions.

"Please," I begged him, "let me speak to *Monsieur le Commissaire*; this is all just a mistake. I haven't done anything wrong."

To my surprise, my request was granted. I found myself

standing in front of an uninterested balding man who half-listened to me as he read the newspaper.

"I am not a criminal," I explained. "I haven't done any harm to anybody."

No response.

"Please," I said, "just let me stay in this room, close to the heater."

The *commissaire* continued reading.

I waited, unmoving, while the guard who had accompanied me scratched his head trying to decide whether or not to haul me back to my cell. He cleared his throat.

Taking the hint, the *commissaire* (without looking up from his reading) waved a hand toward the corner of the room. I curled up there and stared at the guard for a few seconds, until he decided to leave me alone and go away.

I stayed there in the corner all day, keeping quiet so I didn't bother anybody who might decide to send me back to the wretched cell.

Around half past five an officer came over and squatted down next to me on the floor.

"Who are you?" he asked. "What are you doing in here instead of the cells?"

"I'm nobody important. Just an artist. There's been a little mistake."

"What does he say, Georges?" asked another officer, leaning on the *commissaire's* desk and looking me over with casual interest.

"He says he's an artist."

"Artist? Let's see him draw something."

They brought me a pencil and some paper, and I drew a portrait for each of them. I worked slowly, careful not to make a mistake because there was no eraser.

I handed over my sketches and the two agents inspected them. They showed each other their likenesses and beamed giant grins. These were men who liked to see themselves.

Georges left the office and returned a few moments later with some other officers and sat them down in front of me. I had customers.

I charged a few franks for each sketch and the officers kept coming every couple of hours. Some even brought in their wives and children to have me do a family portrait. Often there were gifts of a little cheese or some wine, and many of the agents gave me a little more money than I asked for.

In two weeks' time I had saved enough to pay for the ticket and the fine I owed. When I returned to the railway station the same sergeant who had been there the day I was arrested was on duty. He recognized me.

"Haven't you been in jail?" he asked. "How did you get the money?"

The officer who had escorted me explained.

"Well then," smiled the sergeant, *"Bonne chance!"*

Soon I was back on the train with a paid ticket, on my way to Holland by way of Belgium. To get to Belgium, French citizens didn't need visas, only valid passports. Of course, I had neither, but as usual I was prepared with a good excuse.

"You see," I explained, "I am a sailor, and I lost my ship in Le Havre."

"Lost your ship?" one of the officers asked. There were about four officers who had boarded to check passports.

"I got drunk and my ship sailed for Antwerp without me."

The officer suppressed a little smile. "Well," he said, "you shouldn't drink so much. If the Belgians let you ride, though, I suppose it's OK with us. Good luck."

In Brussels I used the same story, and (mostly because I'd established a precedent by getting the French to let me ride) they agreed to let me stay on the train. I got off in Brussels, where I visited Mr. and Mrs. Isbecque.

Mrs. Isbecque embraced me warmly and kissed me on both cheeks. I told them (with some deliberate omissions) about my adventures in France.

"You should go home to Germany, Walter," Mrs. Isbecque advised me. "There is no way you'll ever make it to America."

"You'll see," I laughed. "Father told me there was no way I'd make it to France!"

Mr. Isbecque smiled at me.

I spent the night with them, and there was no more talk of going home to Germany.

The following day I got back on the train, this time headed for Amsterdam, Holland. I was feeling confident as we chugged along, and despite Mrs. Isbecque's numerous warnings that I'd need a visa to get through the border, I was relaxed as we came to a gentle stop in Roosendaal.

We were all asked to get off the train, and we were herded like sheep (even worse—sheep with luggage) through a narrow causeway that opened on a number of desks belonging to Customs and Immigration.

This time I explained, "I got drunk in Antwerp and lost my ship. I have all my belongings aboard. Please, I have to get to Amsterdam."

The Dutch customs officer rubbed his red nose with one bony finger and said, "You will have to go back to Antwerp and get a visa. Without it we will not let you in. So sorry." And then, as if he were trying to apologize but didn't know how, he added "Try to watch your drinks."

The customs agent looked anxiously behind me at the growing line of people and quickly shooed me away.

I sat down on a bench and balled my fists in my lap as I

stared at the floor in disgust. *Why were there so many borders in the world?*

The crowds thinned out and eventually dissipated into nothingness and silence. Gone too were the customs agents and other officials, off somewhere perhaps for lunch or just a rest before the next trains came in.

I felt sick. How cruel was fate, and how inane to have stopped me here, of all places, in harmless *Holland.*

And then of course I realized that I was, more or less, exactly where I'd intended to be. I wasn't to Amsterdam yet, but I was over the border and free in Holland!

I looked about me, fearful that I'd discover some sort of barrier trapping me within the train station, but there was none. With the agents gone there was nothing to stop me from walking out into the open streets of Roosendaal. Within minutes I had found myself a ride with a truck driver headed east.

I rode with this great bear of a man for perhaps three quarters of an hour until we reached the next city, where I convinced a young physician to let me continue with him to Rotterdam in his little roadster. Along the way we had a flat tire, and the doctor got out to have a look but seemed confounded by the whole concept of car trouble. I offered to help, and we were soon bumping along again on the spare.

"I can't thank you enough, sir," he said to me. "I was afraid we'd be stuck there all day. I wish there was something I could do for you in return for your help with the tire."

"You've done me quite a favor already today," I said. "Thanks again for the ride."

That seemed to satisfy him only partly. We rode on in silence for a few minutes.

"So what's in Rotterdam?" he asked.

"Excuse me?"

"Rotterdam. Why do you want to go to Rotterdam? Family?"

"No. Actually, I'm trying to get to Amsterdam. I lost my ship and I'm trying to catch up with it. I suppose I'll find another ride to take me the rest of the way from Rotterdam."

"That's quite a way by car."

"Maybe I'll take two cars."

"Why don't you let me buy you a train ticket?"

That suited me fine.

The doctor waited with me at the train station and waved good-bye to me as I left, wishing me luck. I almost felt sorry for deceiving him with my story about losing my ship, but then, I don't suppose I would have gotten transport to Amsterdam if I'd told the truth. Being truthful isn't always the best way to get where you're going.

When I got to Amsterdam I found Barbara almost immediately. I took my pencils to a local bar and found her already set up with a little easel and making quite a lot of money.

Things in Amsterdam were just as they were in Le Havre. We worked together, pooling our money, and in the evenings we made love and drank cheap wine. We eventually decided to move to Rotterdam, where there was more traffic and more sailors.

For a portrait I charged two packs of cigarettes, which I sold on the black market for eight guilders each. Eating was never a problem because food was plentiful on the docked ships and all we had to do for a meal was to ask for it. The sailors liked us and were generous with their cigarettes and with gifts of clothing. Life was easy.

One afternoon Barbara asked me to accompany her to the police station to get a food stamp—groceries and other personal items were still being rationed out that way.

There was a line at the desk where they gave out the

stamps, and Barbara and I meandered slowly through it and talked. I noticed the officer at the counter staring at us as we got closer to him. Perhaps it was the accent; something about us had attracted his attention.

He stamped Barbara's book without looking at it; his eyes were fastened on my own. I tried to look away, but I felt awkward and naked. Somehow he knew that something was not as it should be.

"What do you want?" he asked me.

"Nothing," I responded casually, "I just came along to accompany the lady."

"What's your nationality?" he asked.

"American."

"Show me your papers."

The people in line behind me now were starting to take an interest in what was going on.

"I don't have my papers with me. I left them on my ship."

He thought he had me.

"What ship?" he asked.

"The *Prince of Wales*," I said, smiling. It was an American vessel I knew to be in port at the time.

I turned to go but the officer reached over the counter and caught hold of me by the wrist. I knew better than to struggle with him right in the middle of the police station.

He hauled me into a little office and sent another officer over to take care of the food stamps. I was shoved into a chair while, to my horror, the policeman called the port authority.

"What is your name?" he asked me while he waited for his call to go through.

"John Smith," I said.

Someone picked up on the other end of the line and my

officer asked if there was a John Smith on the crew list for the *Prince of Wales.*

There was a tense moment of silence, me waiting for the officer, waiting for the port authority, waiting on John Smith.

"I see."

He hung up. John Smith was not on the crew list.

I was escorted to a superior officer, and to him I explained that I was French and had come to Holland illegally.

Five minutes later I was in jail.

There was no way out except to leave the country—Barbara had to come and pay a fine before they would even deport me. A day later, in Roosendaal, I was put on a train and sent back to Belgium.

Fortunately, it was still legal for me to stay in Belgium (as long as they thought I was a Frenchman), so I didn't get sent all the way back to Paris. I stepped off the train in Brussels, ate lunch, and turned around to start hitchhiking to Holland. Two days later I was back in Rotterdam.

I couldn't find Barbara, so I started asking around to see if anyone knew where she was. As I wandered the port area from bar to bar I happened upon the same police officer who had escorted me to the train a few days earlier. He looked right at me, paused, and then went about his business. Perhaps he assumed that I'd gotten a visa and returned legally. More likely he was just not interested in another drive to Roosendaal. Still, my luck seemed to be running out in Rotterdam.

I heard from a bartender at the International Seamen's Club that Barbara had left for Amsterdam. She'd left a note for me, asking me to find her there.

It was autumn of 1948, and I had tired of my many adventures in Europe. In Amsterdam I caught up with Barbara, who told me that she was thinking of visiting Germany for a while. She wanted me to go with her.

I had accumulated a good amount of money, and this I kept in a large wooden box under my bed. As Barbara sat naked in my little hotel room one evening and talked to me about her plans of going to Germany, I retrieved the box, opened it, and removed most of what I had saved.

"Here," I said, "go to Duesseldorf and give this money to my parents." I gave her the address. "I can't go home yet, but don't worry. We'll see each other again soon."

That was the last time I saw Barbara.

I heard from my parents years later that she had gone to visit them, but that she had come penniless and had borrowed from them. So it goes.

Stowaway

I **returned** to Antwerp. In those days you could board just about any ship that was docked. If you had sailor friends aboard you could even sleep there for a few nights if there was an empty bunk. Staying aboard ship was good for business—it was certainly the best way to put oneself in contact with a lot of sailors (excluding, of course, working in a brothel).

On the Argentine ship *El Gaucho* I found many customers for my portraits and many friends as well. Two officers gave me the names of their families in Montevideo, Uruguay, and Buenos Aires, Argentina. I thought about stowing away on *El Gaucho*, but the captain must have been suspicious because he asked me to leave after I'd been hanging around for a few days.

At the post office a letter arrived from my father:

> Walter,
>   Your mother is anticipating your return for Christmas—she has baked special cookies. She needs you badly.

You won't be able to get out of Europe; we expect
you home soon.

To which I offered the equally curt reply:

Dear Father,
    If I don't find a ship that will take me to America
within two weeks, I promise to be home for Christmas.

I considered this letter a masterpiece. It was a promise I
would keep if I had to. In the meantime it would quiet my
mother's unrest and motivate me to work harder to find a
way across the Atlantic. My father's pessimism had ignited a
fire in me that would not be doused. Somehow, I was going
to get aboard a ship headed for America.

With *El Gaucho* gone, I turned my attentions toward the
Parkhaven, a seventy-five-hundred-ton Dutch coal freighter
that may have been one of the oldest vessels on the seven
seas. According to the local papers, she'd be sailing for Brazil
in less than a week.

I made friends with Kris, an assistant engineer. From him I
learned that most of the crew members were Dutch and had
gone to Holland to visit family. That meant that a lot of bunks
were empty on the ship, and that I could sleep there and
make friends among the crew members.

I met another Walter, a cook. Walter and I spent a lot of
time talking to each other in the evenings, when the ship was
empty and lifeless and immensely hollow, and I confided in
him my plans to stow away. I asked for his help.

"Well, first you'll need some place to hide. Once the crew
starts living on board again there won't be a corner of the
ship anywhere that isn't bustling all day long. You'll need a

place to sleep, too. Most of these bunks will fill up again soon, but I think I might know of a place that will do."

I smiled at him. "Thank you, my friend."

I said my good-byes to all my friends among the crew the day before the ship was set to leave. I disappeared until three in the morning, then I snuck back aboard undetected. Walter met me and led me to an empty bunk tucked away among those of the kitchen helpers. He had had to let a few of his friends in on our little secret, but they were mostly men I'd met before and they didn't mind helping me.

"You just stay here and keep quiet," Walter told me.

"For how long?" I asked.

Walter had no delusions of keeping me safely hidden for the duration of the voyage. "For as long as you can. If you're found out close to the coast, the captain will send for a speedboat to come and pick you up. You'd better stay out of sight until we're past the English coast, understand? It'll be just as bad for me as for you if you get caught, so don't move."

There was a little curtain that could be drawn over each bunk for privacy. After Walter left I pulled mine closed and went to sleep, waiting for our departure.

The next morning the purser came to our cabin and drew my curtain while I lay sleeping. No one bothered to wake me up, but consciousness slowly trickled back into my body as I heard the voices of the men arguing around me.

"Well, I don't really have any choice. I'll have to report him to the captain."

"Of course you have a choice. You either report him or you don't. He's not hurting anything. We've got an extra bunk. Why not leave him be?"

There were four or five men badgering the purser to leave

me alone. He turned around to have another look at me and discovered that I was awake. That seemed to be just enough embarrassment to convince him to let me stay.

"But you'll have to find some other place to hide," he reminded me as he left, "and if it ever comes up you'll have to tell the captain that I never saw you."

After the scare with the purser, Walter was also of the opinion that I needed a better place to hide. Late at night I was taken to the most remote recess of the ship, the compartment where the propeller shaft passed through the hull and into the water. This was an alien world, a bulb of strangeness within the ship that soaked the magic out of the vessel and made an offering to the sea, coercing it into letting metal float on water. I lowered myself slowly down a small ladder with iron rungs until my legs contacted a loose network of wet and slimy ropes—sinews in the belly of the whale.

There was no longer enough light to make out shapes or even the dimensions of the room. I sat on the ropes and listened to the water rising and falling rhythmically a few inches below my feet. I couldn't guess the size of my cell, and in the darkness those two days and nights I imagined more than once as I awoke from some uncomfortable half-sleep that I was back again in Germany in solitary confinement.

When we had reached the open sea my companions came to retrieve me and threw open the hatch. They had to haul me out with great effort—all of my limbs had gone to sleep.

I was taken immediately to the captain. He would find out soon enough, and the sooner he was aware of me the less wrathful he would be.

As it was he cursed repeatedly and stormed about the room yelling and asking questions. He seemed surprised when I told him that I was French and more surprised that I spoke Dutch. He was suspicious.

"Say 's-*Gravenhage*."

"What?"

" 's-*Gravenhage*. It's a city near the Hague. Say it."

" 's-*Gravenhage*."

"You're no Frenchman," he concluded. "No Frenchman could pronounce that word correctly."

I gave him the story about being Alsatian and explained that I could speak both French and German.

"As well as Dutch?" he asked.

"Much better."

"Let me see your papers."

I showed him what little documentation I had. Unfortunately, I had long since lost my seaman's book in La Rochelle.

"I will turn you over to the immigration authorities in the next port," he said. "In the meantime, you will have to work."

He called for the ship's stewart, who gave me linen, towels, and soap and assigned me to the same bunk I had used before, near Walter and my friends from the kitchen.

I thought that perhaps I would be assigned to work with these men as a cook's assistant or doing some similar work, but I soon discovered that I was not so fortunate.

"This is Lovey, he's the other coal trimmer on your shift. You two will be working together from 4 A.M. to 8 A.M. and 4 P.M. to 8 P.M. every day."

The chief engineer paused, looked from me to Lovey and back again. "Lovey will explain the particulars."

Lovey was a small but solid black man from Curacao. He had a slow, deep voice that seemed to come from his mouth like some organic thing, a giant tree taking root. I liked him instantly.

Our first few days were spent on deck, removing a great heap of coal that had been piled there. Once we'd leveled that black mass to nothing more than a stain we were sent below deck, where we threw shovelfuls of coal from our side of the boiler room to the other for the firemen who would fill the furnaces. It was tremendous work. I would scoop out the coal with my wide shovel, using it as a counterbalance to keep me steady as I timed my motions against the rocking of the boat before emptying it at the other end. The sway of the sea was a wretched metronome that regulated us and kept us forever dancing in the room with our black and heavy partners.

In the afternoons I began to do some artwork. I drew portraits and copied photos of loved ones. I even decorated the menus for our Christmas dinner. Most importantly, though, I secretly worked for several days on a portrait of the captain, which I presented to him on his birthday on the seventh of January. It had been signed by all the crew members.

A few days later I was called to the bridge.

"Claude," he said, smiling kindly, "I want to help you out. I'll take you to Montevideo and I want you to keep quiet in Vitoria. You have some place you can stay there where you won't attract too much attention?"

I told him that I had a rich uncle in Montevideo who would be expecting me.

"Good. Now go on and get to work. Your shift's about to start."

I thanked the captain profusely and met up with Lovey on his way to the furnace room. I told him the good news.

"The captain say that?" he asked, dubious.

"Every word."

Lovey didn't seem pleased for me.

"Why? What's wrong?" I asked.

"You shouldn't trust him so much, Claude. Probably he just wants you to be at ease so you won't cause any problems. I know the captain, and I tell you he's going to turn you over to the police. I am sorry, my friend, but I have no doubt that he will give you up."

I wasn't going to take any chances.

On January 14, 1949, we pulled into the port of Vitoria, Brazil. I waited until the ship slowed to wait for a local pilot to come aboard to navigate the port channels. When our speed became the child of momentum alone, I jumped and swam.

I had swum perhaps a hundred yards when a police boat skirted past me, doubled back and picked me up. The little boat took me to the port authority.

An interpreter, a son of Germans, was called to help with the interrogation. I was told that I would be taken back to Rio de Janeiro, handed over to Immigration, and sent back to Europe.

I hardly heard a word of what was being said. My mind was filled with the realization that I was standing on Brazilian soil, land separated from my home not by more earth but by a great ocean and a great rift of culture.

"Please," I said. "If you are just going to send me to Rio, why not let me stay on my ship? Why all the complication and the cost of getting me there? I see now that there is no way for me to stay here in Brazil."

I stayed there in the police station for two days while they tried to decide what to do with me. The interpreter seemed to like me (partly, I think, because he admired me for having learned four languages at such an early age) and he convinced the police to give me a little freedom and to help me get back aboard my ship.

The captain was of course furious when he found out what had happened.

"You don't understand, Captain. I can't go back to Europe. I was afraid."

"Why didn't you trust me?"

"I don't know. I just didn't want to take any risks."

The captain stared at me. "Look, Claude. I will help you out. I'm not going to turn you over to the authorities in Montevideo, but you have to do as I say and trust me, understood?"

I nodded.

The New World

We left Vitoria on the sixteenth of January. We arrived in Montevideo six days later. In the captain's quarters I squeezed under a desk and waited in cramped silence while the authorities made a run of the ship. They never even entered the room.

Minutes after the inspection crew had left, the captain was pressing ten Uruguayan pesos into my hand and wishing me well. "You will always be welcome on this ship," he said.

I found myself alone and content wandering the streets of Montevideo. I didn't speak the language, and what money I had wouldn't last long, but I had made it to Uruguay; I had beaten my father.

Then I took one of the letters I'd been given on *El Gaucho* and found my way to the address written on the envelope. A neighbor girl who spoke English was called to act as interpreter. It was strange for me, listening to this little girl tell me that I would, under no circumstances, be allowed to stay in her house. She emphasized that it would be impossible for me to stay in Uruguay without papers.

"You should try to get to Argentina," she advised me.

"There is a large German population there and you will have better luck finding someone to help you."

I realized that I wasn't going to convince the little girl, or rather the woman with whom I was having the circuitous conversation, to let me stay. With a little effort, though, I got her to agree to let me leave a little suitcase with her, which I promised to send for later.

Disappointed but not disillusioned about the potential for new successes in this new world, I returned to the ship and sought out the captain. I found him reading in his quarters.

"I spoke with my uncle on the phone."

"Good. Everything's set then?"

"Not exactly. I need your help."

"Hmm?"

"My uncle moved to Buenos Aires. He wants me to meet him there. Please, take me with you to Argentina."

The captain set down his book and offered me a seat.

"Claude," he said, "I've already told you that you're welcome to come with us wherever we go, but if you sail with us to Argentina I won't let you off the ship in Buenos Aires. The Argentine police are terrible; I can't take that kind of chance."

He paused for a moment, perhaps considering my dilemma. He seemed to have happened upon a solution. "Why don't you forget about your uncle and sign on with the crew? We could use an extra hand."

"I don't know what I'm going to do. I have to get to Buenos Aires."

"I'm sorry, my friend. Why don't you think about it for a few days? I'd love to have you on the ship—you work hard and everyone likes you."

I was feeling frustrated. With my hands in my pockets and my head bent toward the ground, I found my friend Kris and asked him for help.

"You can hide me! You can keep me in the propeller shaft again until we get to Buenos Aires!"

"No, Claude, I *can't*. I'll lose my license."

"Nobody will know about it!"

"Claude, the captain already knows about your little hiding place and he knows that you want to get to Buenos Aires. He'll find you if you stow away again."

"Somewhere else, then! There must be somewhere else I can hide."

And there was. Kris finally agreed to help me, and he asked me to return at three in the morning the night before we were to set sail, just as I had done previously.

Kris led me through a maze of little access tunnels deep in the bowels of the ship. When he had reached the most remote of these he opened a small hatch in the floor that led to a little space under the furnaces.

"It will be hot in there," he said, "better leave your clothes with me."

I disrobed and surrendered my shirt and pants to him, then lowered myself into the little cavity.

"Remember," Kris said, closing the lid to my tiny coffin, "don't move until I come and get you after we've arrived in Buenos Aires."

I lay there in the profound and heavy blackness, unsure at times whether my eyes were open or closed. After a time I heard the ship's horn and knew that about three hours had passed. They had been long hours for me.

It was a twenty-five-hour journey to Argentina, and I grew intensely aware of the passage of time, numbers rolling in my head as I counted the ups and downs of the ship and the slow and steady progress of air drawn in and then pushed out of my lungs. I was afraid to sleep, so I counted and listened to the noises of the ship.

After what seemed a long time I was startled as part of my world, the placental drone of the engines, disappeared. They had shut off the engines.

I was happy at this. I knew that we were close to shore and that the captain had relieved the boat of its drive to let the tugboats have their way with her.

Soon, though, there were different noises. Rasping, banging sounds from overhead.

The firemen were cleaning the furnaces.

With great hoses they sprayed the fireboxes above me, knocking away the accumulated deposits of soot. I was soon covered with a heavy layer of warm, wet ash. This was at first pleasant in some primal way, but soon the temperature became unbearable. I could feel my heart throbbing in my ears, and the weight of the soot on my chest felt like some living thing, a smothering animal come to suck the life out of me.

With supreme effort I pawed my way through the black and weighty sleet as it fell in clumps from above. I pressed myself against the access hatch. It opened, and I pulled myself halfway through before passing out on the floor of the tunnel above.

The firemen revived me with cold water. They were surprised to see what they had thought to be black skin streak away to reveal a white and fair-haired young man. More water, and they recognized me.

"Claude? How did you get here? What were you doing?"

I had almost no energy, but I managed to open my mouth to beg them not to tell the captain.

One of them had left to fetch the chief engineer, who was already coming through the little hatch as my request died on my lips. He looked me over, told me he would have to tell the captain. "He will be very angry with you," he said.

I had come too far to give up so easily. The firemen realized that I was not hurt badly from my stay under the furnace, so they left me a hose and went back to their work while the engineer disappeared to go find the captain. I bolted.

I found my way to the deck, where some of the crew were busying themselves getting ready to come into port. From these men I procured a small rope ladder and dropped it over the edge of the ship. I gathered my energy and climbed down as far as it would take me, then loosed my grip and dropped into the water.

The men on deck were pointing and laughing. Some of them were simply pleased with the spectacle, but others were genuinely cheering for me. One man hollered out that there were sharks, that it was dangerous to swim.

We were at the lip of the River Plate, the giant ribbon of water that separated Buenos Aires and Montevideo. We were still miles from shore, and the port was little more than a glow reflecting off the clouds and a few blinking lights in the distance. I swam toward the lights on the horizon.

Something large and slick slammed into my legs, and for a terrible moment I gritted my teeth and shut my eyes tight in anticipation of the giant ripping bite of a shark.

There was nothing. It must have been a piece of debris of some sort. I kept swimming.

I swam among many vessels, some anchored and waiting for pilots to come and guide them into port, others moored and quiet. Flags in the stern announced their nationality. I picked out a Norwegian ship and started pulling my way through the water toward it.

I was close to shore now, close enough to hear the shouts

of men there yelling at me, telling me that I wasn't allowed to swim here. I waved back to appease them, trying to look confident as if I had a perfectly good reason to have taken a swim in the port waters.

I reached the Norwegian ship and was helped aboard by the deck hands. I was filthy, covered in oil and the stink of the river, but I was welcomed. This ship had already passed through customs and so had no fear of a stowaway. Someone handed me a towel.

"De donde viene?" ("From where are you coming?") a native asked.

I shook my head, indicating that I didn't understand.

"Where did you come from?" someone offered, this time in English.

"There." I pointed to the Parkhaven, a dark shape some miles in the distance. It would be several hours before she would advance on us and moor not far from the Norwegian vessel. Following my finger with their eyes, the crew let out a great cheer and circled around me with shouts of congratulations. I was, for the moment, a hero.

That was January 24, 1949.

I didn't know what was ahead of me in Argentina or in the vast expanse beyond that was North and South America. Staring into the sunrise breaking over the coastal horizon, I could watch light tracing its course over the curve of the world, circling my planet and drawing its luminous fingers over my past and future, over Dusseldorf and Ravensbrueck and France and the ocean and bursting finally in a tendril of white heat over my head here, in Argentina. Behind me lay the corpses of the Holocaust and the curious adventures of my youth.

Ahead of me were fortunes to be made and lost, two

marriages, four children, three Ph.Ds, and years of travel. Occupations would come and go; one day I would work among cattle as a gaucho and the next I would find myself dining with President Lyndon Johnson. Through it all there would be the lovely peace of painting, which would bring me joy as I worked on commission for the Pope and doubly so when I would sit at home and draw the contours of my wife's face.

I don't know how much of that life I would choose for myself and how much of it would come to me through fortune and misfortune and what many would call "blind luck." But I think perhaps I have gone from place to place and time to time with a purpose, though one less formal than most: I have tried to be happy. I was happy that day in Argentina as I watched the sun glowing in gold and silver off the water, and I am happy now, watching that same sun miles distant glimmering on the lake outside my window.

I'm seventy-two now, but I'm not done living. The shining eyes of my new baby daughter, Asai, bring me hope and a new vitality. My future is liquid, and the anticipation of not knowing where it will lead me excites me every day as I get up and part my curtains to look at the world.

About the Author

Walter Meyer now resides in Austin, Texas. He has taught, painted, farmed, and raised horses, to name just a few of his colorful pursuits.